Outpost Kelly

Fire Ant Books

Frontispiece. First Lieutenant Jack R. Siewert, Armor, United States Army, Korea, 1952.

Outpost Kelly

A Tanker's Story

JACK R. SIEWERT

THE UNIVERSITY OF ALABAMA PRESS
Tuscaloosa

Typeface: Goudy and Goudy Sans

∞

The paper on which this book is printed meets the minimum requirements of American
National Standard for Information Sciences-Permanence of Paper for Printed Library
Materials, ANSI Z39.48–1984.

Library of Congress Cataloging-in-Publication Data

Siewert, Jack R., 1924–
Outpost kelly : a tanker's story / Jack R. Siewert.
    p. cm.
"Fire Ant books."
Includes bibliographical references and index.
ISBN-13: 978-0-8173-5341-4 (pbk. : alk. paper)
ISBN-10: 0-8173-5341-0 (alk. paper)
1. Korean War, 1950–1953—Regimental histories—United States. 2. United States. Army.
Infantry Regiment, 15th—History. 3. Korean War, 1950–1953—Campaigns. I. Title.
DS919.S5 2006
951.904'242—dc22

                                                              2006003500

To my children, Craig and Cathy, and to my grandchildren:
Jason, Derek, Jennifer, Matthew, Austin, Rebecca, and Tessa

Oral history and anecdotes are fine,
but some stories are best told in written prose

Contents

Illustrations

MAPS

Foreword

In the study of war there is a tendency to look at the "big picture," reflecting on the role of generals and statesmen or depicting the strategy of nations and the movement of vast armies or armadas. Historians of the Korean War have produced some excellent studies along these lines. Among these reliable narrative studies would be T. R. Fehrenbach's *This Kind of War* and Clay Blair's *The Korean War*. It is important to note, however, that the war one sees as a result of the "big picture" is often a distortion. The vastness of war may be more easily understood by drawing generalizations from its complexities, but the basic realities of a war are really understood only when the events are seen as personal. For, in the final analysis, war is personal. It is fought in a particular place by a particular individual who, for whatever reason, finds that he or she is matched against an enemy in a deadly struggle. It is at the individual level that we acknowledge the difference between what Lawrence LeShan calls the mythic and sensory reality of war. Whereas the mythic reality provides motivation and unity to the cause, it is the sensory reality of the individual that makes it happen. It happens in the face of unquestionable fear and the numbing and overpowering desire for safety.

After the United Nations resumed the offensive in January 1951 and, in doing so, brought the majority of the subsequent Communist counterattacks to a halt, the front stabilized along a line just north of the capital city of Seoul. At this point the war moved into its static phase, that is, a period in which action is identified in terms of limited battalion-size, and sometimes regimental-size, attacks. It had been agreed among the cease-fire negotiators that the armistice line would be the line of contact when the truce became effective. These outpost battles were most often a part of an effort to establish control over a piece of terrain to alter the potential marking of a demilitarized zone. This period is called the "Battle of the Outposts" or sometimes just the "Hill War."

Because of the limited nature of these conflicts, it is easy to allow them to fall into obscurity. Most narrative accounts of the Korean War, for example, use the first two-thirds of the book to describe the first year of the war and try to cover the hundreds of hill and outpost battles in the remaining pages. And yet, nearly half of the 140,000 casualties in the Korean War occurred during the later period. From the standpoint of the men involved, these relatively small-scale firefights were every bit as intense, bloody, and demanding as any in history, and they happened over and over again at places with strange names, such as the Punchbowl, Heartbreak Ridge, the Berlin Complex, and the Hook.

Outpost Kelly was one such place. During the course of the war there were several battles for control of this area. The fight covered in this work occurred in July 1952. Outpost Kelly was located between Outpost Albania and Outpost Tessie about two miles west of the Imjin River and was but one in a series of outposts protecting the UN line. At the time of this account it was the responsibility of the 1st Battalion, 15th Infantry.

Lieutenant Colonel (retired) Jack Siewert has provided us with a fairly detailed account of the July contest. Carefully balancing his memory with more objective sources, the then Lieutenant Siewert has provided a beautifully written story of one such battle.

In his story he addresses a battle both common and unique. It is a common tale because it closely reflects more than a hundred other such battles. These outposts were located in front of the lines to both defend and forewarn the main line of resistance, and they were the subject of attack after attack during the latter period of the war. Outpost Kelly was also unique because each of these battles was different, each reflecting the time and the conditions as well as the enemy involved. The story is also unusual in the fact that we see this conflict through the somewhat different perspective of a tank platoon commander.

In primary intent, the tank is an aggressive weapon designed principally for a battle of movement. But as the war slowed and battles became more focused, the tank took on a quite different role. In this role the usually mobile tank crew was often called on to dig in and use its guns as direct-fire artillery. Siewert has dealt quite easily, almost candidly, with the variety of his assignment as he, and his men, faced the conflicting characteristics of this role. The tanks needed to be taken off-road and moved up through the rising hills until the men reached the point where they had to dig in and sight their weapons. He deals with the difficulties of fighting the weather, from the mammoth task of moving a tank along slippery rain-soaked crest lines to adjusting for the unpredictable behavior of weapons when they are very cold. He helps the reader understand the many planning sessions necessary to coordinate the tank and infantry activities as well as the necessity of maintaining daily duties to keep the men busy.

The author is also able to identify clearly the character of the engagement once it begins: the continuous apprehension of the enemy's potential, the dry anxiety of waiting for something to happen, the complexities of fire missions when the firing begins, and the underlying concerns men feel as they focus on the destruction of one another.

In this case the battle is successful, the tanks and infantry manage to maintain control, and Outpost Kelly remains in UN hands for some time. But it is not a permanent victory; few of the hill battles were. After the outpost has been held for several months, it is attacked again. In September 1952 it became the center of a renewed Communist-UN struggle for control of areas that were considered negotiable. During this time, Outpost Kelly eventually fell to the Chinese and is now located within the North Korean sector.

Dr. Paul M. Edwards
Senior Fellow
Center for the Study of the Korean War

Preface

By definition an outpost is a military detachment thrown out by a halted command to protect against enemy enterprises. Outpost Kelly had been established by the 3rd Infantry Division late in 1951 when Line Jamestown, our most forward position in I Corps during the second Korean winter campaign, had been secured. Line Jamestown was about ten miles north of the thirty-eighth parallel, the disputed dividing line between North and South Korea. Ever since the truce talks had started in July 1951 at Kaesong, this terrain had been heavily contested. Every acre of the battlefield had assumed an unnatural importance as the Chinese Communist forces and the United Nations forces scrambled to gain or hold terrain. Many outposts could be found throughout the 8th Army front, particularly in the western sector. These combat outposts had been established at the conclusion of the Summer-Fall Campaign in October 1951. Up until the very end of the Korean War, the 8th Army constantly struggled to hold and control these outposts. Over a period of a year and a half, battles for these terrain features were repeated over and over again. The fight for Outpost Kelly in July 1952 was but one instance of the innumerable small battles that took place up and down the 8th Army front. In the first nine months of 1952, Kelly was contested three times: 4 February, 28 July, and 17 September. Until the armistice talks were finalized, the fighting for the demarcation line of the demilitarized zone would continue. Improvement of geographical positions was a constant effort. The assumption was that whatever you held the day the armistice was finalized and signed would be the positions that fixed the lines of the demilitarized zone. Meanwhile, neither side intended to surrender or lose any terrain features it already held. For the last two years of the war the conflict seesawed back and forth. Negotiations at the truce talks dictated the major activities on the battlefield.[1] Politics and diplomacy shaped the war.

During the 8th Army defensive period of June–August 1951, the military adopted the patrol base outpost concept. This concept extended the depth of the defense by establishing a series of outposts that were to be defended and held under all circumstances short of a major offensive by the Chinese. Manned by battalion- or regiment-sized units, the advanced bases were frequently miles forward of the main defensive positions. Supporting artillery gave cover and protective fire to the patrol base outpost. Commanders conducted vigorous patrolling to maintain contact with the enemy. The truce talks exerted a strong influence on the defensive posture of the opposing forces during this period of the conflict. At this time, our main position was Line Wyoming, which had previously been an outpost line providing early warning for Line Kansas.

Concern over Chinese intentions and capabilities initiated the resumption of the 8th Army offensive on 18 August 1951. In the eastern sector of the 8th Army line, heavy fighting commenced at the Punchbowl and spread to Heartbreak Ridge and Bloody Ridge. By mid-October the enemy had been ejected from these strongpoints, and 8th Army forces held the high ground. Concurrently, Major General J. W. (Iron Mike) O'Daniel, I Corps commander, submitted a plan to create a new defensive position in the western sector, Line Jamestown. This line was to be about six miles forward of Line Wyoming. Operation Commando began on 3 October 1951, and Line Jamestown was secured on 19 October 1951 (map 1).

On 24 October 1951 the truce negotiations were shifted to Panmunjom. The UN forces placed the issue of the establishment of a demilitarized zone high on the agenda. A line of demarcation was an initial step in creating this zone. For the UN forces, this line was accomplished by the UN Summer–Fall Offensive of 1951, which had advanced the 8th Army positions in both the east and west sectors. The significance of these aggressive moves was not lost on the Chinese and was instrumen-

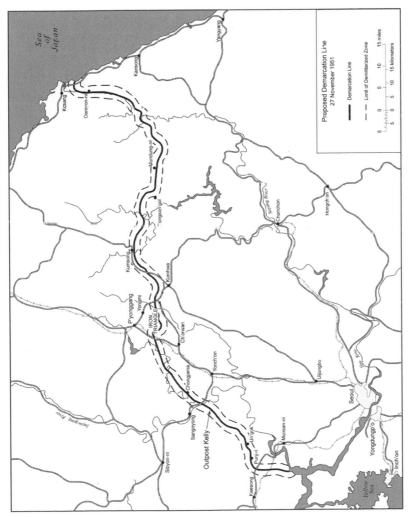

Map 1. Location of Outpost Kelly as related to the 8th Army front line and proposed demilitarized zone, 27 November 1951 (MLR, main line of resistance; MSR, main supply route). (Adapted from the original created by the Defense Mapping Agency Topographic Center. See Walter G. Hermes, *Truce Tent and Fighting Front*, map IV.)

tal in bringing the Chinese to serious discussions at the truce table. At this stage, 12 November 1951, Lieutenant General Matthew B. Ridgway, UN forces commander, directed Lieutenant General James A. Van Fleet, 8th Army commander, to assume an "active defense."[2]

The 8th Army immediately started the consolidation of their newly won positions. Following one of the principles of "active defense," the army suspended large-scale operations. They also followed other principles, including seizing and holding the most defensible terrain along the present main line of resistance; acquiring outposts by offensive action limited to division or smaller units; and using patrols, raids, and ambushes to maintain contact with the enemy. The patrol base outpost system was supplanted by the combat outpost concept. These two concepts contrasted sharply. Whereas the patrol base outpost had been located far forward of the main line of resistance and manned by battalion- or regiment-sized units, the combat outpost was manned by platoon- and company-sized units close to the defensive line. The combat outpost was expected to provide early warning of an enemy attack and then to withdraw, using delaying action tactics as the enemy force advanced.[3] Outpost Kelly was a combat outpost.

The 3rd Infantry Division occupied and held the outpost. The position was about sixteen hundred yards in front of our main line of resistance and was manned by a reinforced platoon of infantry. The fortified area of the hilltop was entrenched, surrounded by barbwire and concertina, and several approaches were mined. There were no trees or shrubs. The total area of the hilltop, which was a slightly rounded dome, was about one acre.

As a hill, Outpost Kelly was obscure and unimportant, being dominated by the surrounding terrain. As an outpost, however, it was to become the focal point of the entire 3rd Infantry Division in the last days of July 1952.

Acknowledgments

This book covers events that took place in the 3rd Infantry Division in Korea, 1951–1952. The core of the story is the loss and retaking of Outpost Kelly in July 1952. I have depended heavily on my personal recollection of events that led up to and occurred on Kelly. In this regard, the dialogue found in the story has been reconstructed as served by my memory; the intent and sense of the dialogue is accurate.

Early on in this writing it became evident that I needed help from many sources. Official U.S. Army documents were obtained from the National Archives and Records Administration, College Park, Maryland, and from the National Personnel Records Center, St. Louis, Missouri. Without these documents it would have been impossible to untangle the cascade of events occurring almost simultaneously during the fighting on 28–31 July 1952.

I am indebted to the many people who generously contributed thoughtful comments and counsel that improved the structure, detail, and accuracy of the story. Special thanks go to John E. Jochem and his wife, Jeanne, for their support and advice. Contributions to understanding the ebb and flow of the combat were generously given by members of the 15th Infantry Regiment. Their recollections and reflections enhanced the integrity of the story of what took place on Outpost Kelly. Of great assistance in this regard were Colonel Sherwin Arculis, Major John T. Burke, Sergeant First Class Theodore A. Cook, and Master Sergeant Henry H. Burke.

1
Reconnaissance Up Front

Korean terrain presents unique problems for the passage of tracked vehicles, particularly in the mountains. Narrow defiles, steep slopes, bottomless rice paddies, ice-covered trails and roads, streams and rivers that cannot be forded, traffic congestion, and a host of other hostile conditions catalog the problems of moving a tank in Korea. A tank platoon leader quickly learns that it is prudent to make a route reconnaissance, time and circumstances permitting, prior to committing his tanks to a motor march. In my case I commanded a platoon of M-46 tanks. At forty-eight tons the M-46, the finest tank in the world, was a formidable machine of war. It was twenty-eight feet long, twelve feet wide, and nine feet high. Much of the weight could be attributed to the armor protection; the front of the hull and the turret each had a thickness of four inches of steel. The Continental V-12, 810-horsepower engine used gasoline in prodigious quantities—three gallons of gas to the mile. The 233-gallon fuel tank gave the M-46 a radius of action of seventy miles before refueling. The tank could climb a thirty-one degree slope and could ford four feet of water. On level terrain it could move at thirty miles per hour. Seventy rounds of ammunition were stowed in the fighting compartment for the 90m/m cannon. The small arms mounted on the tank included a caliber .50 machine gun and two caliber .30 machine guns. The M-46 required a lot of care and attention; a five-man crew operated the tank.

It was 13 July 1952, and Captain Jim Barrett, commanding officer

(CO), C (Charlie) Company, 64th Tank Battalion, had given me my marching orders. A map reconnaissance was the first order of business. Jointly, Barrett and I completed a map study of the area my platoon and I were to report to the following day.

The task my platoon had been given was relatively simple, almost routine. I was to report to the CO, 2nd Battalion, 7th Infantry Regiment, 3rd Infantry Division, to be attached under operational control for the purpose of relieving disabled tanks of the 7th Tank Company. The term "operational control" meant that my platoon would become a combat element of the 7th Infantry Regiment; administratively, the platoon would still be carried on the "Morning Report" of Charlie Company. The disabled tanks were to be repaired and returned in a few days, at which time my platoon would be released from operational control and we would return to Charlie Company. The area I was going into was the west flank of the 3rd Infantry Division, held by the 7th Infantry Regiment. Next to our flank was the British 1st Commonwealth Division. The opposing forces were the Chinese.

My goal today was twofold: to examine the route the tanks would follow, with emphasis on potential problem areas, and to coordinate the transfer procedures for my platoon to replace a platoon of the 7th Tank Company, 7th Infantry Regiment. My map study indicated that I had been in this area back in November 1951. There had been heavy fighting then for control of Hill 355, Little Gibraltar, and Charlie Company, 64th Tank Battalion, had been placed in a blocking position at a nearby ford on the Imjin River from 23 to 26 November 1951. In the event the enemy penetrated to that point in our lines, Charlie Company was to deny them the use of the ford. The route I planned to take tomorrow was a distance of about six miles between the Charlie Company bivouac area and the headquarters of the 2nd Battalion, 7th Infantry Regiment. There the details would be firmed up for my platoon of five tanks to move forward and occupy the positions to be vacated by the tanks of the 7th Tank Company.

Much had changed since last November. I did not recognize any features of the current road. Eight months earlier this road had been a narrow mountain trail scarcely capable of handling quarter-ton truck (jeep) traffic. Today the road was wide enough for trucks to pass in opposite

Figure 1. Bottom of camouflaged road, main supply route, leading into 2nd Battalion, 7th Infantry Regiment area.

directions; it was well graded, had good culverts, and was even ditched in the appropriate places. The Army Corps of Engineers had created a very good road.

As the quarter-ton rose to the top of a long grade, I could see a large billboardlike sign at the side of the road. I told Sergeant Davis, my driver, to slow down so we could read the sign. The sign stated: DANGER. YOU ARE UNDER ENEMY OBSERVATION FOR THE NEXT 500 YARDS. DANGER. A huge canopy of camouflage netting covered the down-sloping road; it was draped and supported high enough to clear a tank with the radio antennas down. It extended almost to the bottom of the hill. The netting looked awfully thin; I could look right through it and see the surrounding terrain with no problem (figure 1). Did this netting really conceal our movement from the enemy? My eyes focused on the commanding terrain feature to the north, Hill 317. I estimated it to be about two and one-half miles away. It was occupied, and held, by the enemy.

Up to now Sergeant Davis and I had been involved in a relatively quiet ride in the Korean countryside on a warm, cloudless day. Now we were abruptly back in the war. I considered this new hazard for a moment.

"Davis, if a round lands behind us, uphill, I want you to 'How-Able' [phonetic alphabet for H-A, which was an abbreviation for 'haul-ass'] down this hill as fast as this quarter-ton will take us. If the round is in front, drive into the ditch to the right, and we'll take cover. Understand?"

Davis responded with a nod of his head and a snappy, "Yes, sir!"

Frankly, I did not know whether this was the best plan or whether our maneuver should have been reversed. The point was that the hazard had been recognized and a contingency plan made to accommodate it.

We reached the bottom of the hill without event. A small roadside sign pointed the way to the 2nd Battalion, 7th Infantry Regiment. Even without the sign, the jumble of hastily laid telephone wire, both on poles and lying along the side of the road, pointed to the command post (CP). I made a mental note to remember that the movement of my tanks through here would have to be done carefully to avoid tearing up the telephone wire.

The administrative area of the battalion was in a small valley surrounded by ridges. The CP was in a medium-sized utility tent with the sides rolled up for ventilation, light, and access to the numerous slit trenches surrounding the tent. I was received by the battalion executive officer, Major Lovis Caudell. He said he was expecting me and explained that the battalion commander was at a regimental briefing and that I would see him tomorrow. My mission, he stated, would be the same as that of the 7th Tank Company platoon—to support ground combat operations by direct fire from the tanks. The fire support was delivered from fixed dug-in positions located on a ridge top, part of the main line of resistance (MLR) that was also occupied by the 7th Infantry Regiment Heavy Mortar Company. The infantry line companies were also disposed along the MLR. The whole battalion was on the line. The frontage to be covered was so extensive that all the combat assets were committed to meet the mission responsibilities.

The major used a detailed wall map, 1 to 50,000 scale, covered with clear plastic and marked with grease pencil, to describe the tactical situation graphically. The 7th Infantry Regiment left flank was also the 3rd Infantry Division left flank. This boundary was shared with the 1st British Commonwealth Division situated to the immediate west. Running through the 7th Infantry Regiment area was the Imjin River. The Greek Expeditionary Battalion held the east flank, and that boundary was shared with the 65th Infantry Regiment to the immediate east. So, facing north, the regimental alignment reading west to east was 2nd, 3rd, and Greek battalions, with the 1st Battalion in regimental reserve. There were numerous outposts along the regimental frontage; the 2nd Battalion was responsible for Outposts Cavite, Kelly, Tessie, Nick, and Betty. Outpost Nori was a 3rd Battalion responsibility. Not all the outposts were manned at the same time. The most commanding terrain feature in the area was Hill 355, Little Gibraltar, which we held; the next most significant feature was Hill 317 to the north, held by the Chinese. The road I had come in on was the main supply route (MSR) and served the regimental area from the west flank boundary to the Imjin River. The opposing force was the 348th Regiment, 116th Division, 39th Chinese Communist Forces army (maps 2 and 3).

"That's about it," the major concluded. "The two disabled M-46 tanks on Hill 199 will be down by tomorrow. You can plan to occupy their positions when you get here in the morning. There has been a delay in getting the engineers to build the road, but by tomorrow the recovery operations will be completed."

My mind had been going pretty fast absorbing this briefing, but now I thought, Whoa! Wait a minute! Did he mean two tanks and two positions only? Up to now, with the information available to me, I had been planning to bring the 2nd Platoon, five tanks, forward and deploy them to bring the enemy under the fire of my 90m/m guns. At my briefing this morning Captain Barrett had stated that a platoon of the 7th Tank Company had to be taken off the line for rear-echelon maintenance. The 64th Tank Battalion had been directed by G-3 (Operations), 3rd Infantry Division, to provide a replacement platoon on a temporary basis until the repairs were completed, a project that was estimated to take several days. Ultimately, the mission reached me. Further details were to be finalized at the 2nd Battalion.

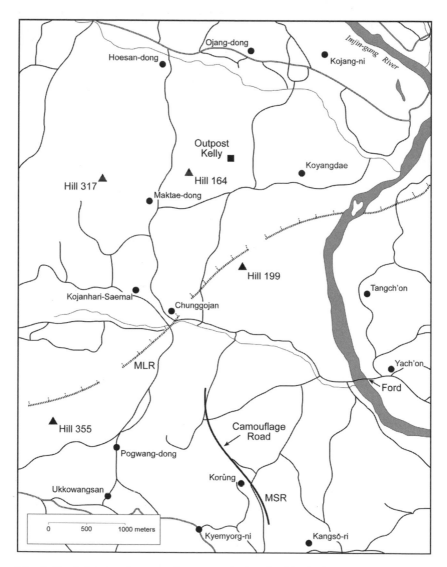

Map 2. Detail showing the terrain features involved in the fight for Outpost Kelly. Map is adapted from Map Sheet 6528 II, scale 1:50,000, 1,000 meter grid, Majon-Ni, Korea. (From the 64th Engineer Base Topographical Battalion, U.S. Army, November 1951.)

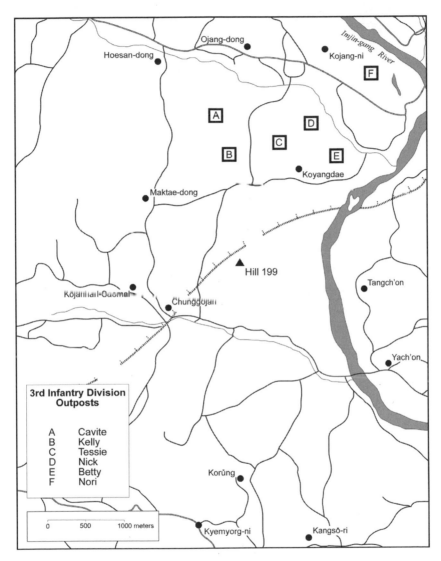

Map 3. Detail showing the outposts in the 3rd Infantry Division sector relevant to Outpost Kelly. Map is adapted from Map Sheet 6528 II, scale 1:50,000, 1,000 meter grid, Majon-Ni, Korea. (From the 64th Engineer Base Topographical Battalion, U.S. Army, November 1951.)

"Major," I said, "are there only two firing positions?"

"Yes," he replied, "but they are dug in—revetted for hull defilade—and each position has its own bunker."

"Any chance of developing more firing positions so I can get all five of my tanks up there?" I asked.

"Possibly," he responded. "Take a look around when you get up on the ridge. If you think you can squeeze more tanks in, we'll see what can be done. You will meet the CO, Major Crain, tomorrow. Plan on being here at 0900 hours."

This concluded the briefing, and I was turned over to the S-4 (the logistics officer) to work out the logistic details of joining the 2nd Battalion, 7th Infantry Regiment. The S-4 was well acquainted with the needs of a tank platoon, so the arrangements for billeting, mess, medical support, fuel, ammunition requisitioning, and communications were quickly settled. I reflected briefly on the major change in my plans and expectations—only two firing positions. Somehow, through channels, the requirement for two tanks had been translated into a platoon. Now what? Should I bring two tanks forward and leave three in bivouac at Charlie Company? Or was it best to keep the platoon together and bring everybody up front regardless of how I might be able to deploy them? I elected to bring the whole platoon forward for several reasons: most important was maintaining unit integrity and developing teamwork; second was preparing for the unexpected; and, third, I figured that in an emergency, five tanks were better than two. And maybe there was room on the ridge for five tanks. Accordingly, I arranged for the light section (two tanks, including mine) to be on top of the hill and for the heavy section (three tanks with the platoon sergeant) to be at the foot. For logistics the entire platoon would be attached to Headquarters Company, 2nd Battalion, which was near the battalion CP.

The next order of business was to see what the top of Hill 199 looked like (figure 2). Davis and I drove the short distance to the road that led to the top and discovered that a tank recovery vehicle blocked it. The marking on the vehicle identified the 703rd Ordnance Company. We parked, dismounted, and walked up the hill; it was a 350-yard climb up a steep, narrow, dirt road just wide enough for a tank. Road dust, like fine powder, puffed and billowed with each step. Near the top, recovery

Figure 7 Hill 199, looking north from the camouflaged road. The headquarters for the 2nd Battalion is in left center of photo. The Imjin River is on the extreme right.

operations were under way for the disabled tanks. We paused to watch the activity. One tank was in the road facing backward downhill. We learned that both tanks had transmission problems, which clearly made this an awkward recovery. In my mind I could visualize the complexities of attaching forty-eight tons of immobile tank to a tank recovery vehicle positioned on a steep, narrow grade. The recovery crew was in for a long, hot, sweaty day coupled with some high anxiety. The second tank was farther up the road, still parked in its revetment. I could find no officers in sight, which bothered me because this recovery operation demonstrated a high level of complexity and hazard dealing with very expensive combat vehicles. I left Davis to observe the recovery operations; as a tanker he could learn something about accomplishing a difficult task. My interest was in the vacated tank position about thirty yards farther uphill to the left.

Standing in the revetment, looking north, I was pleased with the field of fire from this position. In place, only the tank turret would be above ground level. To the immediate front, about one hundred yards away, ran a ridge parallel to the one I was on. That ridge out there was the forward edge of the MLR. I could see a service trail on the side facing me, with bunkers both above and below the trail. I noticed communication trenches leading up the slope and then disappearing over the ridgeline to the military crest where the fighting trenches were located. Also to the front beyond the MLR, through a shallow saddle in the ridge, I could see Outpost Kelly. I looked through my ten-power binoculars, but I could not detect any activity on Kelly. I estimated the range to be about fifteen hundred yards from where I was standing. Outpost Tessie, which was to the right, did not show any activity either. I could not see Outposts Nick, Betty, and Nori, also to the right, because the ridge to the front masked my view. The dominating terrain feature was Hill 317, to my left front, about a mile and a half away. Enemy held, it overlooked our MLR; I did not see any hostile activity. A quick tour of the adjacent bunker showed it to be well made. The immediate area had all the signs of an abrupt departure; it was trashy and needed "policing up," or restoring it to correct standards. Far to the right, beyond the second tank, I could see the Heavy Mortar Company area; I decided I would visit that location tomorrow after getting settled in. My survey up to this point clearly showed that this hilltop offered no more positions to place additional tanks. I would have to shelve that idea.

I rejoined Davis. "How are they doing here?" A glance showed nothing much had changed.

"There are too many bosses there." Sergeant Harold D. Davis shook his head in a vigorous negative manner. With Davis, attitude and aptitude made a congenial blend. He was nineteen years old but had already made sergeant. Of medium height and wiry, he had the right physique for the tight confines of a tank. And he was cool and controlled under pressure, a trait he had exhibited a number of times. As a tank driver he could not learn much more; he knew the operation and maintenance of the engine and transmission, suspension, electrical, and hydraulic systems. I suspect he knew as much about the unit-level maintenance and repair of the tank as did our company mechanic. The "21" tank (the numerical designation was based on the platoon and tank number; in this case, the "2" indicated the 2nd Platoon, and the "1" indicated that it was the first of the five tanks; the "22" tank meant 2nd Platoon, second tank, and so on) was always ready for the mission. Mental preparation for your personal response to the stress of combat is an important element of being a soldier. Davis handled this like many nineteen-year-olds; he knew he was immortal. As the driver of an M-46, he knew he was invincible. Every task was done briskly; his driving was done with dash and verve. At times he had to be reined in to ensure we got to our destination without a calamity. He was a real hell-for-leather cavalryman.

We approached the second tank position. It was about forty yards to the right of the position I had just visited. The M-46 tank was still in hull defilade in the revetment. No personnel were present; they were probably assisting with the recovery operations on the tank down the road. The field of fire here was as good as the other position. Again, the bunker looked sound and certainly large enough for a five-man tank crew. As we were leaving, Davis said, "Lieutenant, did you notice this excavation work and road to the rear of the tank? The recovery guys were talking about it—they said this tank peeled a track, left side, and couldn't get it back on until the engineers built a road under the tank! Had to be a hell of a job."

Sure enough, the area was scarred by heavy-equipment tracks, and there was an unusual quantity of heavy timbers on hand. I had thought they were for bunker building, but now I realized they were used to shore up the M-46 tank during the building of the road or, more precisely, the hardstand. It had to have been a tough job. The major's remark about a road-building delay at my briefing an hour ago now became clear. Other things were beginning to become clear as well. Two inoperable tanks; could that be a coincidence? I could only speculate. With vehicles, particularly track-laying vehicles, constant attention to maintenance is an axiom you live by. Life is a series of cause-and-effect relationships. Speculation again, but could inept maintenance be the reason my platoon was being sent forward to support the 7th Infantry Regiment?

As Davis and I left Hill 199, the recovery activity was well under way. The tank recovery vehicle was inching its way backward up the hill to the disabled tank. It was shortly after noon.

"Davis," I said, "let's find that Headquarters Company mess tent and get a sample of the chow we'll be eating for the next few days."

2
Close and Join

Our motor march from the Charlie Company bivouac area to the 2nd Battalion was just over six miles. White Front Bridge, over the Imjin River, was a new trestle-bent structure that replaced the old pontoon bridge. Although the bridge was rated at a capacity to handle the forty-eight-ton weight of an M-46 tank, we still crossed the structure gingerly. Only one tank was permitted to cross at one time; all crew members except the tank commander and driver had to dismount and walk—the same way we proceeded through a minefield. The idea was to approach a potential hazard with the view of minimizing casualties. A river route was available, but I rejected the option yesterday because the march was much longer and required fording the Imjin River at three locations. The depth of the river at any of the three fords could be a serious obstacle for a tank, and at the moment I had no sure knowledge of the condition of the Imjin. The route with the fewest obstacles was the preferred way to approach tank movement in Korea.

Of the many barriers to tank travel, the worst were minefields and ice. Both these obstacles were deadly. Fortunately, Charlie Company, and my platoon, faced only one minefield during my tour of duty. It was our own minefield, unmarked on the maps we had, and the consequence was merely rerouting our column and extending our motor march. Charlie Company was not so fortunate with snow and ice conditions. Late in

November 1951, Charlie Company took up a blocking position on the Imjin River. We had been given a defensive mission to support the 7th Infantry Regiment holding Hill 355, Little Gibraltar. The west flank of the 3rd Infantry Division was under heavy assault by the Chinese. The ford was to the immediate rear of the MLR and was to be defended should the enemy effect a breakthrough. The fighting for Hill 355 lasted several days, and during this time our tanks made numerous trips along the sandy, beachlike banks of the Imjin River. Some parts of the river route, however, were narrow passages where one side of the trail fell away sharply. We discovered that the routine drive over a narrow defile covered with ice became an experience in sustained anxiety.

The tracks of a tank are made up of individual shoes, flexibly connected to each other. The normal, all-purpose shoe was made of a rubberlike composition with a cleatlike design. This shoe worked well on paved and dirt roads and trails and provided a ground-grabbing surface for open fields, desert, hills, and obstacles. But, on an ice-covered surface, the rubber-composition shoe lacked traction. When a tank is sliding toward the edge of a trail that drops off sharply, the event causes your mind to focus very intently on the situation at hand.

The fight for Hill 355 was resolved in our favor, and the temporary blocking position of Charlie Company became a permanent bivouac on a bend of the Imjin River. As the winter wore on, the tank drivers became more skillful at negotiating icy surfaces. Still, coming on a slick surface unexpectedly had a chilling effect on the driver and crew. In many instances an icy patch of road would be handled as though it were a minefield. The tank crew, less the driver and tank commander, would dismount and follow the tank on foot until the passage had been safely made. As events turned out, our company of tanks would not get through the winter without a loss.

During the second week of February 1952, two platoons from Charlie Company were sent forward to support the 15th Infantry Regiment. Operation Snare (code name Clam-Up at headquarters, 8th Army) was to commence on 10 February 1952 beginning at last light; the operation was a self-imposed silence throughout the 8th Army and was to last for five days. The goal was to draw the Chinese out of their defenses and inflict casualties. During this period the 3rd Infantry Division, inert and dormant, would await the expected Chinese probes and then ambush the enemy. All activity of the division normally visible to the enemy would be concealed. The outposts to the front of the division would be pulled in. Vehicle traffic on roads that could be seen by the Chinese would be discontinued. Smoke from fires would be eliminated. Noise from vehicles and machines would be suppressed. All activity along the MLR would be conducted out of sight of the enemy. Artillery, mortars, and aircraft flying over the front lines would cease operation. All patrols were to be canceled.

The two platoons from Charlie Company arrived on the east bank of the Imjin River two days before the operation was to commence. Our firing positions were located on a low ridge about two hundred yards behind the MLR trenches that overlooked the Imjin River. Immediately across the river was a large valley that extended to the west for miles. On the west bank of the Imjin was Outpost Nori. With the exception of the outpost, the Chinese held everything to our direct front and to our northwest.

Our two tank platoons, abreast, took up firing positions on the ridge. My platoon was on the right flank, and the terrain permitted my tanks to back down off the ridge into a full defilade position. This gave my tanks the concealment dictated by the requirements of Operation Snare. The tanks of First Lieutenant George W. Woodard, platoon leader, 3rd Platoon, were bivouacked in a hollow to the left of the firing positions. The tank crews of the two platoons erected "hex" (hexagonal) tents and set up light housekeeping to the immediate rear of the tanks. They then dug latrines and sanitary fills and established a telephone line between my platoon and A Company, 15th Infantry Regiment, located nearby. Should enemy artillery or mortars shell the area, we would take cover in the tanks.

On 10 February 1952 the platoons conducted live firing to establish the range to various potential targets in the valley to our front. Lined up on the ridge, each tank crew fired a few 90m/m high-explosive (HE) rounds. Crews checked radio communications within platoons and between platoons. Once Operation Snare commenced, radio traffic would cease. By mid-afternoon both platoons had completed their firing missions and began to retire to their concealed bivouac areas. My tank was still in its firing position on the ridge when a shout went up close by: "A tank is on fire!"

My first reaction was the feeling of a deep chill and a question— whose tank? I stood up in the turret and looked to my left. About a hundred yards away a thick black column of smoke rose in the sky. What the hell was going on? I wondered. I dismounted from the tank and dashed over to the fire. The scene was gut wrenching. A tank from George Woodard's 3rd Platoon was upside down in a ravine located to the rear of the ridge from which we had just been firing. The tank was totally engulfed in flames, and a rivulet of fire coursed down the ravine. Gasoline from the gas tank poured out onto the ground and stoked the fire. The rubber of the track shoes had already started to burn, emitting an oily black smoke.

As I approached George, I had one immediate thought: are there sur- vivors from the tank crew? George, visibly shaken, was giving instruc- tions to men of his platoon. I asked him about the crew of the burning tank. His response came in a controlled and deliberate manner. Of the five crewmen, four were accounted for, and none were seriously injured. The fifth crewman was missing and was presumed to be in the burning tank. The thought of being trapped in a burning tank made my stomach turn. There was anguish and hopelessness reflected in George's face. Fighting the fire was far beyond the means at hand, and saving the trapped crewman was a consideration that was beyond human capabili- ties. The burning tank represented a worst-case scenario.

Concern regarding the expected explosion of the ammunition aboard the tank dictated that all personnel be moved a safe distance away. Here, out of sight of the burning tank, the tragedy was reconstructed.

Woodard's "31" tank had led the move off the ridge to the concealed area in the hollow. As the tanks moved along the spine of the ridge, in file, the tracks compacted the snow covering the frozen earth. With the passage of each tank, the track marks became progressively glazed with ice. The last tank in Woodard's column lost traction and started to slip sideways down the back slope of the ridge. Forty-eight tons of tank, out of control, picked up speed as it moved ponderously to the lip of the ravine and then slid forty yards on a relatively shallow slope. When the track on the left side went over the edge, the tank overturned and crashed to the bottom of the ravine fifteen feet below. Gasoline escaped from the gas tank and ignited.

Interviews with the tank crewmen filled in the events that followed. With the tank upside down, the bow gunner fell out. He then assisted the driver, whose legs were caught, out of the driver's compartment. In the turret, the tank commander and the gunner were able to scramble out of the loader's hatch. This part of the turret top had, luckily, come to rest several feet above the ravine floor, leaving a clearance. The whereabouts of the fifth crewman, Corporal Wesley G. Herrmann, were unknown.

The tank burned for two days. We expected the 90m/m HE rounds to explode, but only the white phosphorous (WP) went off. The HE rounds did not detonate but "cooked off" as low-order explosions. After three or four days, when the tank had cooled down somewhat and was safe, various visitors arrived to inspect the vehicle. Ordnance personnel and 3rd Infantry Division staff officers came to the scene to assess the damage and report on the incident. Quartermaster personnel officially confirmed that Corporal Herrmann died as the result of being crushed to death. His body was found halfway out of the tank commander's hatch. Although this was a tragic loss and a grisly death, to many it was a relief to know he had not been trapped in the turret and burned alive.

Operation Snare did not achieve any spectacular results. The Chinese stayed close to their lines and sent out only small reconnaissance patrols. The Chinese briefly occupied Outpost Nori, but they had departed by the time the operation was concluded.

The loss of our tank brought home the hazards of a combat environment. Enemy fire was not the only thing that could kill you. Something as ordinary as a snow-covered ridge could be the foe.

That cold day in February was a direct contrast to the conditions today. This July day was hot, and the dust our tank column kicked up was impressive. Five tanks in a column present a very businesslike appearance. The platoon mechanic in the quarter-ton brought up the rear. I stretched the road-march interval to one hundred yards between tanks to improve the visibility for the drivers. A little wind would have helped a lot; as it was, the dust just hung in low clouds along the side of the road. We halted at the camouflage net section of the road leading down into the 2nd Battalion area. Over the radio net I repeated my earlier instructions: only one tank should be under the camouflage netting at one time, and I would tell each tank when to start down the hill. In this way the movement of the tanks would be random rather than systematic and predictable. There is little point to presenting a lucrative target to hostile artillery fire. Although the camouflage netting would conceal the tanks, the moving dust cloud rising through the netting would alert enemy observers to vehicle traffic. As it turned out we negotiated the hill without incident and soon arrived at our prearranged assembly area near the 2nd Battalion CP. About one hour had passed since we left the Charlie Company bivouac area. It was 0830 hours; we were early.

Before reporting to the battalion commander, I reviewed with my platoon sergeant the "motor stables" I expected him to conduct. This routine maintenance was performed to ensure the mechanical soundness of the tanks, and it included topping off the gas tanks. An M-46 got less than one half mile to the gallon, and you were never sure where your next supply point would be found.

At the CP tent entrance I was met by the battalion sergeant major. "You're Lieutenant Siewert?" he asked.

"Yes, Sergeant Major, I'm here to report to your commanding officer."

"Major Crain is expecting you." The sergeant major gave me a kind of half smile and said, "We could hear you coming in."

I could almost read his mind: tanks are noisy, they create a lot of dust, they attract artillery fire, and they tear up telephone wire. Basically, these are things an infantryman dislikes. On the other side of the coin, each tank had a 90m/m cannon, a caliber .50 machine gun, and two caliber .30 machine guns. Basically, these are things an infantryman likes if the tanks are supporting him. On the way to the CP I had noticed bunker-building activity at a nearby hillside and asked, "New bunkers?"

"We're improving on the old ones. This CP tent is temporary. They can't finish those new bunkers soon enough for me. We've been getting a lot of H&I [harassing and interdiction] fire from Joe Chink, usually at night. The new bunkers will be a lot more substantial than this tent. I'll see if the CO is ready to see you."

There was no delay. I was ushered into the CO's office by the major who had briefed me yesterday.

"Sir! Lieutenant Siewert reporting for duty as ordered." I held my salute until the CO returned it.

"Please stand at ease, Lieutenant. Any problems getting here?"

"No, sir. My whole platoon is present. I've closed and joined."

"Looks like you had a dusty march getting here. How long have you been with the 64th Tank Battalion?" he asked.

This question, I knew, was directed at discovering how much exposure I had to combat operations. I was an unknown quantity. He had a legitimate reason for probing. My problem, now, was how detailed should be my response.

"Major Crain, I joined Charlie Company last fall. I was just in time for the fight for Hill 355 in November. My platoon was in a blocking position at the river ford on the Imjin a thousand yards to the east of this CP." I decided to stop my resume at this point. If he needed more details I figured he would ask.

"Well, Major Caudell briefed you on the mission. I understand that you have your logistic support organized with my S-4. I don't believe I have anything to add. Do you have any questions? Any requirements?"

"I have a request, sir. I want to do some firing to establish range to targets and get my range cards in order. Who do you wish me to coordinate with?"

"Siewert, you're on a par with my company commanders. You report directly to me. All your orders will come from my staff or me. When you want to conduct fire missions, you will coordinate that activity with my S-3 [Operations officer]. Have you met my Operations officer, Captain Hornstein? Well, Major Caudell will make sure that you meet him before you leave the CP. Anything else?"

"No, sir," I replied.

"Oh! One other thing. The 703rd Ordnance Company advised me that the tanks to be repaired are to be back in a week. Looks like your stay will be short. I'm glad to have you with the 2nd Battalion."

"Thank you, sir. I'm pleased to be here."

I came to attention, saluted, and Major Caudell and I exited the office.

These orders and mission suited me just fine. It appeared that I was to have a free hand, no strings attached, in engaging enemy targets. Armor is primarily an offensive weapon. I had been thoroughly trained and schooled in this doctrine and had been practicing, to the extent possible, the tactics of the offense for the past eight months. Armor is all about the initiative, carrying the fight to the enemy with mobility and shock action. Sitting stationary on a hill reduced the effectiveness of the tank by eliminating its mobility; the effect of surprise was gone. But the element of shock action was still there. A salvo of 90m/m high-explosive cannon fire on a target was devastating. While here with the 2nd Battalion, my platoon would work on taking the enemy under fire.

The S-3, Captain David H. Hornstein, went over the deployment of the regimental line companies in general and companies of the 2nd Battalion in particular. The specific location of the Chinese deployment was sketchy. Our reconnaissance and combat patrols were active, but there had been no recent penetration of the Chinese lines, so detailed intelligence of positions was lacking. With the exception of H&I fire, enemy activity was almost dormant. He strongly emphasized one point: we were facing Chinese forces, not North Koreans, and these troops were well trained, well disciplined, and well led. We were facing the Chinese 348th Regiment; they were first-rate fighting men.[1] This did not come as news to me; I had been fighting these Chinese for the last eight months. Max Hastings, in The Korean War, has cited a Commonwealth Division report that makes a similar point: "The Chinese infantryman is well-trained, well-equipped and efficient. . . . He is an excellent night fighter, very brave with good morale and good at finding his way in the confusion of battle. His limitations are due to his lack of equipment and communications. The Chinese are prepared to take casualties and can therefore patrol in strength. There is little doubt that the war in Korea has been fought to suit the Chinese. His limitations in communications, his lack of air support and absence of heavy equipment and vehicles would make him a very vulnerable opponent in a war of movement."[2] Well, we were no longer in a war of movement. It was clear that the S-3 thought the Chinese infantryman was in his element. The targets he showed me fell into the category of "suspected" positions. As far as firing, he just wanted me to coordinate with his Operations section to ensure that no operational or safety conflict existed, such as a patrol scouting the enemy lines. As the presentation and our discussion developed, I gathered that he believed that if I could hurt the Chinese, more power to me.

First Day, 0900 Hours

I left my platoon sergeant at the foot of Hill 199 with the "23," "24," and "25" tanks. He was situated on a good hardstand away from vehicle traffic. The three tank crews would set up our five-man cloth hex tents for billeting, dig individual slit trenches, and perform interior guard for the tank perimeter, one guard per tank during the hours of darkness. The 2nd Battalion was installing a hard-wire line, with EE-8 field telephones, between the two tank areas. My tank position on the hilltop was already connected to the battalion switchboard. I planned to bring the quarter-ton to the top of the hill if I could find a place to park it. My platoon sergeant would join me on Hill 199 on a daily basis, or I would come down to the tank perimeter, and we would plan the daily activities of the platoon. I told the sergeant that I would call him for a radio check on the SCR-508, the tank-to-tank radio, when I got to the top of the hill.

I mounted to the tank turret, put on my headset, and said to Davis, "O.K., let's take Two-One [the phonetic "21"] up." The "22" tank followed as we slowly rose up the hill.

Up front and on the line again, I thought. Quick mental images went through my mind of earlier missions. A combat environment demands both the mental preparation for a potential fight and the alertness for pending action. Even so, the violence and abruptness of combat can be startling—and deadly.

~

On 10 January 1952 Charlie Company, 64th Tank Battalion, was given the mission of sending two platoons forward to support the 3rd Battalion, 65th Infantry Regiment, from Puerto Rico. Intelligence had indicated that on this night, the Chinese were to launch an attack in the 3rd Battalion sector of the MLR. The direct support fire from two platoons of tanks would be used to augment the normal supporting artillery and mortar fire. Our CO, First Lieutenant Clay T. Buckingham, selected my platoon and that of Second Lieutenant Stan Joltan for the mission. As the senior officer, I was placed in charge of the assignment. We left our company bivouac area on the Imjin River at 1500 hours. Starting at this late hour of the day was cause for concern. By the time our two platoons got forward, there would not be much daylight left to reconnoiter the terrain and deploy our tanks.

Most of our route was on the MSR, and both Stan and I were familiar with the road. Our expected problem was traffic congestion. We knew our road-march speed would be slow. What we did not expect was the attrition the cold weather would have on our tank column. Only seven tanks left the bivouac area; in the other three, the crews could not start their engines. These three would join the main column when they became operational. As events transpired, only four tanks eventually arrived at the 3rd Battalion. It was now 1600 hours, we had traveled eight miles, and three tanks had experienced mechanical failures on the march.

Two of the three tanks had the same problem—the transmission oil cooler fan shaft had failed. This was a common malfunction, most pronounced in winter driving. Rapid acceleration, "gunning" the engine, would cause the shaft to shear and break in half. Without the oil cooler fan working, the transmission became inoperable. Driver training emphasized avoiding rapid acceleration of the engine, but in many instances this was not possible. A tank stopped on a steep road frequently needed high engine revolutions per minute to move forward. A stronger, larger diameter shaft eventually solved the broken shaft problem, but in January 1952 the problem was ever present.

Our four-tank column ended up on a small, narrow trail at a gap in the ridgeline occupied by the 3rd Battalion, 65th Infantry Regiment. A deserted hamlet, Mago-Ri, was close by. The trail led north and opened into a valley. On our right the ridgeline dropped sharply to the trail. On our left was a small frozen rice paddy. Still farther to the west, beyond the paddy, the ridgeline commenced again. I could see infantry bunkers along the foot of the ridge in both directions. Entrenched riflemen were situated nearby. Our tank column blocked the narrow trail; obviously, we could not remain here. I had two choices. About a quarter of a mile to the rear we had passed a wide area in the trail where we could park.

To the immediate front, just forward of the riflemen, the trail widened with room for deployment of our four tanks. I elected to take the forward position.

In short order the battalion commander showed up, explained his situation, and described how he expected the tanks to provide support. Then, on foot, he led me along the trail into the valley. We were well in front of the MLR. Briefly, his plan was to have the tanks act in a blocking position on the MLR where we were presently parked. Then, on call, we were to move forward to where we were standing and place flanking fire on the Chinese assaulting the ridgeline. Searchlights would be employed to provide artificial moonlight and illuminate the battlefield. An outpost about one thousand yards forward of the MLR was to be relieved and manned after darkness fell.

It was a straightforward plan, and with the frozen terrain the maneuvering of the tanks would not be a problem. At night, however, movement beyond the MLR without an infantry screen was a problem. I explained my concern of the lack of visibility in a buttoned-up tank at night. The battalion commander assured me that a platoon of riflemen would accompany the tanks forward if we needed to move beyond the MLR. I was satisfied with the arrangement. In the back of my mind, however, I had another concern. My platoon had not engaged in any night firing activity, either in a training role or in combat. Stan's platoon was in the same condition. I rationalized this situation in the category of "on-the-job training." Our blocking position was organized in a diamond-shaped formation so that each tank could provide covering fire for every other tank. My two tanks were on the west side of the trail, and Joltan's were on the east. The "21" tank was foremost, facing north, and was about thirty yards from Joltan's lead tank. The remaining tanks were also situated about thirty yards apart. We set up our hex tents to the rear of each tank and settled in for a cold winter evening. A communications team brought me a field telephone, which connected our tanks to the 3rd Battalion headquarters. Guards were posted in the turret of each tank; the tour of duty was one hour.

About 2330 hours a platoon of 3rd Battalion riflemen made their way northward past our tank position to the outpost. It was a strange sight. The men were strolling at a leisurely pace and were strung out over one hundred yards of trail. They made no attempt to modulate their voices as they conversed in Spanish. I found it difficult to detect a military formation in this seemingly carefree band. As they disappeared into the valley, I noticed that the night visibility was quite good. The light from the moon reflected off the snow-covered ground and produced a scene of contrasting shadow and relative brightness. Later, riflemen of the relieved platoon, returning from the outpost, drifted through our area in small groups.

At 0200, 11 January 1952, I made a communication check with the 3rd Battalion headquarters. No unusual enemy activity had been observed, and I was told that the temperature was ten degrees Fahrenheit and that my crewmen were to take precautions against frostbite. I made one last tour of the guards in my two tanks and alerted my platoon sergeant, Sergeant First Class Tilghman, to take over the role of duty officer for the remainder of the night. I talked briefly with the guard in the "21" tank, Private First Class Theodore F. Edwards, our platoon mechanic; Ted and I both agreed that it was a very cold night. I noted he was armed with my M2 carbine, a gun capable of full automatic fire, in addition to the caliber .50 machine gun mounted on the turret top. Back in the tent everyone was asleep. The small gasoline-fueled space heater was working well. I removed my winter cap and parka, got out of my bulbous-toed, winter-insulated "Mickey Mouse" boots (so called because of their resemblance to the shoes worn by the cartoon character), unbuckled my pistol belt, and crawled into my sleeping bag. With the exception of the parka and boots, I was fully dressed. I lay there for a moment collecting my thoughts about the events of the day.

Suddenly, full automatic fire erupted outside the tent. I was startled from my daydreaming—what was happening? Two very loud explosions shattered the air as I scrambled from my sleeping bag. More automatic fire sounded as I grabbed my pistol belt and lunged to the tent entrance. Sergeant John Wise, my gunner, and I exited the tent together. Outside, the deep cold hit my face. Alert and peering into the night, Wise and I strained to see or hear what was going on. Silence. I took note that we were crouching by the five-gallon gas can that fed the space heater in the tent. This was a poor location with the prospect of bullets flying around. There was stirring in the tent behind us, then a loud, anguished cry from the tank turret: "They shot the gun out of my hands—where are the grenades?" It was Ted's voice. He repeated the query, with his shout bordering on hysteria. I could detect no movement or sound in the vicinity of the tank, which was about five yards to my left front.

"John," I said, "we're going to break for the tank together. You go up the left side, get in the turret, and take care of Ted. No grenades! I'm going to take the right side."

We broke for the tank together at a run. I was at a crouch when I turned the corner at the right rear of the tank next to the sprocket. Pistol extended, hammer back, I found empty space—no one was there. The only sound was Ted, who was still shouting about the carbine being shot out of his hands. Stare as I might, I could not see any movement in our perimeter or down the trail. I became aware of stirring and activity at the other tanks. Stan Joltan ran up and asked what was going on. I briefly told him what I knew and then said we were going on full alert. We would man the tanks, start the engines, and stand by for whatever was coming next. I reasoned that this assault could be the prelude to the expected Chinese attack. Stan suggested that I put on my parka and boots.

My debriefing of Ted was a little disjointed because he was thoroughly shaken-up by the episode. All I could get from him was that a small group, four or five people, had come from the north along the trail. Ted thought, on first impression, that they were stragglers from the 65th Infantry Regiment. He challenged the group, and they responded with small-arms fire. He returned the fire until the carbine jammed, at which time he ducked into the turret and cleared the stoppage. When he re-emerged from the turret, someone shot the carbine out of his hands. At this point he started shouting for assistance.

I had the telephone moved from the tent to the tank turret, and I called the 3rd Battalion headquarters. A duty officer answered, and I explained our situation. I requested that a reconnaissance team be sent immediately to scout the trail to discover any other plans the Chinese might have. The team, part of the Patrol and Ambush Platoon, arrived shortly, and I briefed the English-speaking team leader. They deployed, and twenty minutes later they returned with a negative report—nothing had been seen or heard. No sooner had they left our tank perimeter than a fusillade of automatic-weapons fire, with tracers, came pouring down the trail into our tank area. The four tank crews buttoned-up their respective tanks and waited out the storm of fire. We realized that it was friendly fire and that the source was the outpost to the north. I got on the phone again and reported that we were taking friendly fire. A short time later the firing stopped. This was getting to be one hell of a night. As events turned out, the expected Chinese assault never materialized.

At dawn the four tank crews met at the "21" tank, formed a skirmish line perpendicular to the trail, and moved forward. The purpose was to inspect the area for anything we might have missed during the hours of darkness. There was a lot to be found. Four paces to the right front of the "21" tank, in tall grass, lay a dead Chinese soldier. He had been hit twice in the sternum, apparently died instantly, and was lying on his back with his feet facing the tank. He was wearing a quilted cotton suit and tennis sneakers with no socks. The sneakers and lack of socks made a strong impression on me; this guy had to be one tough son of a bitch to handle winter conditions dressed in that manner. He was armed with a U.S. M2 carbine, just like the one that had been shot out of Ted's hands. The gun was jammed with a spent cartridge case in the chamber, which the weapon had failed to extract. Vegetation directly in front of the tank had been blown away in two places, apparently by antitank grenades identical to a third unexploded antitank grenade found on the left side of the tank two paces from the "21" tank hex tent. The Chinese antitank grenades were made with a large amount of explosive in the form of a shaped charge designed to penetrate armor; it also had a very powerful concussion effect. The "21" crew and I had escaped serious injury or death due to a defective enemy weapon.

As we proceeded, we found even more. Both antenna masts mounted on the top of the turret had been hit by small-arms fire about one foot above the turret top. We found one mast, about three-quarters of an inch in diameter, shot in half, and the other had a neat half-round hole piercing the shaft. This was testimony to the volume of small-arms fire directed at the tank by the Chinese patrol. We found my carbine, the one Ted used, in several pieces. An enemy bullet had struck the barrel band, a metal band that holds the barrel and receiver to the wooden stock. The gun had literally disassembled itself in Ted's hands.

Multiple bullets fired from below had hit the tank commander's hatch cover, which had been in the locked open position. The periscope ring, mounted in the center of the hatch cover, would no longer rotate because the ring was jammed with bullet fragments. The bulletproof glass vision blocks on the right side of the cupola were pockmarked from bullet fragments. There was a bullet splash mark dead center on the cupola ring. Had Ted's body been even slightly out of the turret when that bullet ricocheted off the ring, he would surely have been a casualty. Finally, we found the trail littered with Chinese safe-conduct passes. The pass was intended to persuade UN forces to desert and join the Communist forces.

Later that morning I took the time to reflect on the events of the encounter with the Chinese patrol. Many disturbing, unanswered elements remained to be examined, and we had lessons to be learned. First, why did the other three tank guards fail to fire and support Ted when the assault started? When debriefed, each guard had the identical response—no time to react, the encounter was too short lived. A rational answer, but was it the real one? I had to agree that the fight had been of short duration. Sergeant Wise and I reconstructed our actions to establish an estimate of the time length of the fight. We agreed that about ten seconds had elapsed from our hearing the first full automatic firing to our exiting the tent. By the time we were out of the tent, the Chinese patrol had departed the area. The encounter had been under ten seconds in duration. Second, why did two U.S. M2 carbines, one in the hands of a dead Chinese soldier and the other in the hands of a live U.S. soldier, fail to operate? It was almost certain that the jammed carbine saved Ted's life by causing him to duck into the turret while a storm of automatic fire flew over the turret top. Third, why were the Chinese carrying antitank grenades, a cumbersome weapon, and distributing safe-conduct passes at the same time? What kind of a patrol was that? Were they expecting to run into tanks? Fourth, why did the antitank grenade fail to explode by the hex tent? An entire tank crew could easily have become casualties had that grenade detonated.

There were a number of imponderables related to the encounter, but one element stood out in my mind—the element of chance, pure luck. A jammed gun and an unexploded grenade represented the difference between life and death. Close combat at the platoon level, I concluded, was a crapshoot.

Private First Class Edwards demonstrated all the highly regarded attributes of the U.S. soldier. His actions showed dedication and commitment to the safekeeping of his comrades. He manned his post as a guard in an exemplary manner and confronted the enemy in a courageous way. Two weeks after the fight, at a special company formation at Charlie Company, 64th Tank Battalion, Private First Class Edwards was awarded the Bronze Star Medal for Valor.

~

Over the last eight months of combat I had developed a mind-set that was substantially different from the day I set foot in Korea at the Pusan harbor. Initially, as a Regular Army officer, I believed my attitude toward the enemy should be professionally objective. In carrying the will and interests of the U.S. government to the enemy, I thought it was my duty to make the enemy conform to our plans and goals. He would either surrender or die. I had resolved to execute the will of my government firmly and dispassionately. This high-minded goal had fallen by the wayside as my exposure to combat had accumulated. My attitude toward the enemy had become very subjective. Now, approaching the top of Hill 199, the motto of the 3rd Ranger Company kept repeating itself in my head: "Die Bastards, Die!—Die Bastards, Die!—Die . . ."[3]

The "21" tank was in skillful hands; Sergeant Davis slid the vehicle carefully into the revetment and brought it to a stop. I looked to my right and watched the "22" tank move into its position. The platoon sergeant and I completed the radio check, and I closed down the net until the next scheduled contact. Moving into our new quarters was the next order of business. The platoon had never been billeted in bunkers. For the "21" and "22" crews this would be a new experience. The "21" crew dismounted and started moving sleeping gear and supplies, strapped and tied to the tank, into the bunker. The platoon mechanic would bunk with the crew. Motor stables would come after getting set up in the bunker.

I stood on the right fender side pockets, next to the turret, and looked north. With the engine off it seemed very quiet. I paused briefly; my finger traced the indentation of the bullet splash mark in the cupola ring.

Tomorrow the 2nd Platoon would take the enemy under fire.

3
Hill 199

When I joined the 64th Tank Battalion in November 1951, the front-line area was unsettled. It was difficult to know where our front line ended and no-man's-land began. More than once, on route reconnaissance, I found myself in the contested area between two forces by merely following a road or trail that I thought was within our lines. There were no road signs, no sentries, and no roadblocks to tell you that the "friendlies" were way behind you. You became suspicious when it got quiet and you could not see or hear any activity. The absence of man-made sound would settle over you like a soggy blanket. A battlefield is a lonely place, and when you get beyond the outpost line of resistance (OPLR), it gets really lonely. On bunker-busting "shoot-'em-ups," we would take a platoon or company of tanks far beyond our loosely defined front line and go looking for the enemy, and typically we would find no one. We could maneuver for hours without seeing the enemy or a suitable target. In those days we were dealing with a beaten enemy, men with no will to fight. Our forces could have occupied the terrain we were operating in with relative ease. As Max Hastings has pointed out in strong terms: "In February 1953, Van Fleet handed over command of the Eighth Army in Korea to the veteran paratrooper Maxwell Taylor. The outgoing general disappeared into retirement with bitter complaints that he had been prevented from launching an all-out offensive to drive the Chinese out of Korea once and for all. His frustration was widely shared by other senior officers. It seemed profoundly unsoldierlike to that generation, which had come to maturity in World War II, in which defeat and victory were absolutes, to allow an army to stagnate upon the mountains of Korea, restricted to patrolling."[1]

So, why did our forces not move strongly beyond what came to be called Line Jamestown? The answer, of course, was political and diplomatic, not military. As noted in the preface, the "active defense" order of General Ridgway on 12 November 1951 had brought the 8th Army offensive to a standstill. Only local attacks were permitted. At Panmunjom, the truce negotiations dragged on. From late October into November no agenda items were finalized. In mid-November the UN delegation, in a bid to break the impasse and finalize the armistice, offered a proposal to the Communists. The UN would agree to the current front line becoming the final demarcation line between the opposing forces, provided the rest of the armistice agenda was completed within thirty days. The Communists, under heavy pressure to hold the existing front line, did not delay in accepting this proposal. What was behind this unusually quick response? Max Hastings has succinctly summed up the reaction by the Communist delegation and the subsequent results:

> This was a move designed to show the Communists, and the world, that the UN had no interest in further territorial gains in Korea. It was also intended, of course, to hasten Peking and Pyongyang toward a rapid ending of a war in which Western opinion was becoming increasingly weary. The Communist negotiators hastened to ratify the proposal on November 27. Then for thirty days they talked empty nothings at Panmunjom. And while they talked, immune from major UN military action, on the mountains their armies dug in. Day by day, yard by yard, they sank their trenches and tunnels into the hillsides. For 155 miles from coast to coast of Korea, through December 1951, they created a front of defensive positions, manned by 855,000 men, almost impregnable to artillery fire and assault. Successive lines were interwoven into a fortified belt from fifteen to twenty-five miles in depth. By December 27, when it was amply apparent at Panmunjom that the Com-

munist delegation had merely been playing for time, their armies were dug into positions that, with only minor variations, would form the final armistice line nineteen months later. The Communists could feel entirely satisfied with their progress. They were well aware of the growing war-weariness with Korea among the western democracies. Granted that they had been compelled to forgo the immediate prospect of a military takeover of South Korea, they could hold their existing positions confident that it was most unlikely that the governments providing the UN contingents would tolerate the casualties that would be necessary to break the Chinese line. Peking and Pyongyang, facing the real risk of complete defeat in June 1951, had now achieved a virtual no-lose position.[2]

In thirty days, as Walter Hermes has noted, the duplicity of the Communist delegation had resulted in "firing positions that were practically artillery proof and certainly mortar proof."[3] With the coming of the Second Korean Winter Campaign, both sides were engaged in static position warfare. The truce talks would go on for another year and a half. For the tanks, the days of "shoot and scoot" were long past.

By July 1952, tank tactics were characterized almost exclusively by occupying high ground to obtain good fields of fire. The only maneuvering we did was getting on the high ground. A route reconnaissance usually included walking over the approaches to a ridgeline in order to gauge the ability of a tank to follow the footsteps we were taking. We walked the ground before we committed the tank to the same route. The days of the hell-for-leather dash around the enemy flank, as it was at the Inchon landing and the breakout at the Pusan perimeter in September 1950, was a distant memory. Tank doctrine is predicated on mobility and firepower—shock action. Blitzkrieg, the employment of combined arms, puts tanks in the traditional role of the cavalry with the advantage of having devastating firepower. The ability of tanks to move and shoot, combined with equally mobile infantry and artillery and coupled with air support, was developed and exploited to a high degree in World War II. Early tactical success by the Germans in employing this concept was duplicated later by the Allied armies in successfully concluding the war. The terrain of Europe and the deserts of North Africa were favorable to tank warfare. The mountains of Korea, however, presented substantial problems to the movement of tanks. The static warfare of the last years of the Korean conflict brought an end to tank mobility as a tactical advantage. The tank became a direct-fire support artillery piece located on a hill with a commanding field of fire. Tanks rarely went forward of the MLR. Infantry tactics were characterized by trying to create impregnable trench and bunker systems and well-fortified outposts for early warning. Small pieces of real estate became bargaining chips at the Panmunjom truce talks.

Although the combat activity had gone through a dramatic change from dynamic movement to static trench warfare, the lethality of the battlefield had changed very little. Both sides probed the defenses of the other: combat and reconnaissance patrolling was very active, particularly at night; artillery and mortar fire was a constant threat.

My plan for the remainder of this first day was to get acquainted with the top of Hill 199. While the crews busied themselves with settling into their new quarters, I started my tour. To the immediate left of the "21" tank, the ridgeline narrowed sharply and ran slightly downhill. To the right, between the "21" and the "22" tanks, the terrain showed a marginal possibility to position a tank. It was obvious, however, that a short road would have to be constructed for access to the position. Tanks have a climbing capability, but the hurdles at this site were far beyond the abilities of a tank. Farther to the right, just beyond the "22" tank, was the bunker system for the Heavy Mortar Company. There was no room for additional tank positions on Hill 199. The assessment I made yesterday was confirmed. My concept of having the whole platoon on the hill was scrapped. I would have to think of some other way to get the platoon involved in fire missions.

At the Heavy Mortar Company I found the CO, a first lieutenant, and introduced myself. He was aware of the exchange of tank platoons. We saw no conflict between his mission and mine while sharing the limited space on the hilltop. Logistically, my supply requirements for food, water, ammunition, and fuel would be delivered with his resupply. His 4.2-inch mortar section was situated downhill below the CP. There were several bunkers down there, and the mortars were in sandbagged pits. The CP bunker was large and had an observation port that overlooked

the MLR. This was a rarity because it required tunneling to go from the
rear slope to the front slope of the hill. It represented a lot of digging
effort. The east side of Hill 199 dropped off abruptly beyond the CP and
fell rapidly to the Imjin River.

It was early afternoon when a two-and-one-half-ton truck (6 × 6)
made its way up the road. It was our daily supply drop-off. The truck
delivered food, water, fuel, ammunition, and other supplies, and it carried away the empty fuel and water cans and 90m/m brass casings. The
same truck delivered supplies to the Heavy Mortar Company. Under
normal circumstances, the truck made three trips a day, mainly for food
delivery that arrived in marmite cans, insulated food containers designed to keep the food hot. The crew in the truck comprised Korean
Service Corps (KSC) men with a U.S. infantryman as a supervisor.
The KSCs were not Korean soldiers; they were employed for manual labor wherever it was possible to use them. Typically, they hauled supplies
and built roads and bunkers. The KSCs relieved the infantrymen from
onerous, but necessary, duties. The hard skills, the real dirty work—
fighting—was left to the U.S. infantryman and other 8th Army fighting men.

For the few days the platoon was to be here, I intended to make
the most of my opportunities for tank gunnery exercises. The army personnel rotation system in effect in 1952 created a continuing need at
the unit level for the training of new replacements. There was a constant turnover of tank crew members. The rotation system was based on
points, called constructive months' service (CMS). On accumulating
thirty-six points you were rotated out of Korea and back to the United
States, the land of the big PX (post exchange). You acquired points on
a monthly basis, and the number allocated depended on your location
relative to the combat zone. Four points were awarded if you were up
front on the line. In the division reserve, called the intermediate combat
zone, three points were awarded. Beyond the division rear, to the Korean
shoreline, warranted two points. The rest of the Far East Command
merited one point.[4] Typically, our tank crew members were with their
units about nine months. This was a relatively short time to acquire the
skills needed to perform effectively as a tank crew member. Usually replacements were relatively unskilled due to a short basic training period

and even shorter advanced training. They would arrive at the platoon with the Military Occupation Specialty 3795, Tank Crewman, but they normally could not perform adequately to the standards set by Charlie Company. In Charlie Company each crew member was expected to perform in a competent manner the duties of each position in the tank. Cross training was an ever-ongoing activity. Drivers learned to be gunners, loaders learned to be drivers, and gunners learned to be tank commanders. The goal was to place any man in any position in the tank and expect him to perform well. Teaching the skills to be learned in the time available was a formidable task.

I was ably assisted in this troop-leading enterprise by the presence of Sergeant First Class Charles T. Holt, platoon sergeant. He was Regular Army, had six years' service, and was well schooled in tank tactics. In the army we have a saying: "There is a right way, a wrong way, and the army way." Well, Sergeant First Class Holt was an expert practitioner of the "army way," which was, of course, the precisely correct way—a place for everything and everything in its place. He knew tanks and tank doctrine and troop leading. I do not know whether leaders are born, but if they are, Holt was the epitome of the born leader. He rarely raised his voice when giving instructions or a command; he made his point through command presence. He was an authority figure, and he carried it well. Above all, he was aware of the lethal environment in which the platoon operated. It was this understanding that drove him to work tirelessly to impart his knowledge and skills to the platoon. He knew that training was what led to living to see the next day. With him as second in command, the platoon could not have been better served. In every sense he was the right man in the right place at the right time.

Our gunnery would go against live targets. Well, we hoped they were alive. The intelligence-gathering capability of the S-3 was really very limited. The information provided by the S-3 showed only "suspected" enemy positions. The face of the enemy that my gunners could see was blank. The terrain facing us had no man-made features. All hostile fortification was on the rear slopes of the mountainous peaks and ridges. Basically, our 90m/m tank cannon was a direct-fire, flat-trajectory weapon and was usually expected to hit only what the gunner could see. The artillery and mortars, on the other hand, were high-angle trajectory weapons and could drop their rounds on targets that were behind obstacles and masked to the view of the gunner.

SECOND DAY, 1130 HOURS

This morning, our second day on Hill 199, was to be devoted to establishing our range cards. Range cards are tables of gun elevation and azimuth from the tank to the target; they are normally used for night firing or poor light conditions when the target cannot be seen. We had received our firing mission clearance earlier from the S-3. A map analysis showed that all the targets were less than one and one-half miles away. Hill 317 was the farthest, and it was only twenty-three hundred yards as scaled from my topographical map. The ranges to the targets were to be confirmed by firing HE shells and by observing the strike through the gunner's ten-power telescope. A point to be considered was that in tank gunnery terms, one thousand yards is considered to be point-blank range. For targets up to one thousand yards, the gunner would make no elevation adjustment; he would just lay the telescope crosshair on the target and fire.

Both the "21" and "22" tanks spent the morning firing at "suspected" targets. Aiming stakes were set so that the tank, if moved, could be returned to the revetment with precise alignment. Then, by referring to the previously established range cards, we started very accurate indirect firing. Outpost Kelly was marked and listed at sixteen hundred yards but, obviously, was not fired at.

The gunnery went smoothly, but it was hot work in the late morning sun. My attention was on Sergeant Donald J. Gardner, my gunner. He was very good at his job, and as I watched, the phrase "highly professional" came to mind. At that moment he was establishing his range cards, and my focus was on his deft handling of the gunners quadrant. The quadrant, an essential element in laying the gun for a particular elevation, is coupled with the traversing mechanism to set the proper azimuth to the target. Hand and eye coordination are the basic ingredients of a gunner's skills. Gardner had honed these skills to a high level of proficiency. His manner was methodical, almost detached, yet quick and sure. This physical trait also carried over into his personality. Cheerful and outgoing, he approached the problems that life presented to him in an analytical way. At twenty years of age he had created a philosophy that permitted him to dissect a problem coolly into its fundamental parts and then to solve each part in turn until the problem as a whole had been reconciled. You could almost see the wheels turning in his head. Whatever he turned his hand to in the future, I was sure he had the mental tools to cope with anything life set in his path.

In the fighting compartment, the turret, air circulation was poor, and the smell of sweat mixed with that of gunpowder. We had no wasted space. Sitting in the tank commander's seat, head and chest out of the turret, I had to be careful not to kick the gunner in the back of his head. The front center of the turret was taken up with the breech-and-recoil mechanism of the 90m/m cannon. On the left side of the cannon was a coaxially mounted caliber .30 machine gun. Coaxially mounted to the right of the cannon was the ten-power gunner's telescope. On the inside left wall of the turret was the ready rack of ten 90m/m rounds available to the loader for instant use. The rear of the turret, behind me, was filled with radio equipment. We had two radios: the SCR-508 provided communication between tanks in the platoon and with other platoons in the company and company headquarters; the SCR-300 was used for contact with units other than the tanks, the infantry for instance. Immediately behind me was a drawer of hand grenades. Ammunition for the cannon was stowed beneath the floor of the compartment in the ammunition wells. The basic load of seventy rounds was made up of four types of ammunition: HE, WP, shot, and hypershot. We had little expectation of fighting against tanks, so the bulk of our rounds were HE for use against personnel and such relatively soft targets as bunkers and trenches. The intercom system permitted voice communication between crew members; a switch on my intercom control allowed me to talk to the other tanks in my platoon. Mounted on the tank commander's hatch cover was a periscope that could be rotated three hundred and sixty degrees for visibility when the tank was closed up. The inside of a tank turret was a poor location for a person who suffered from claustrophobia.

Outside, each shot stirred up a large cloud of dust from the muzzle blast. Both the "21" and "22" tanks completed their range cards for the list of targets that had been provided by the S-3. I shut down firing operations for the day. As I climbed out of the turret I wondered how the Chinese had reacted to this "wake-up call."

THIRD DAY, 0900 HOURS

On the third day I decided to try out the gunnery exercise that Sergeant First Class Holt and I had worked up the prior evening. Although I could not get any more tanks on Hill 199, I still wanted to get the whole platoon involved in gunnery. The idea was to use the "21" and the "22" tanks as firing platforms for competition between all five crews. One crew selected a target unknown to the other crew and fired a round of HE. The burst of the round then became the target for the competing crew who, in turn, engaged that target as quickly as it could. Time, in seconds, was measured between the first and second shots; the winning crew was the one with the shortest reaction time. A typical fire command was as follows: "Gunner, HE, target burst, left front, twelve hundred, fire!"—the tank commander's instruction to his crew.

The loader pulled a forty-four-pound HE round from the ready rack on the turret wall, rammed the round into the cannon breech, and shouted, "Up!"

As the gunner centered his telescope on the target, he finalized his elevation and azimuth corrections, stomped on the firing pedal, and shouted, "On the way!"

"Crack!" The muzzle blast was deafening as a twenty-pound projectile of HE was sent at more than twice the speed of sound to its target twelve hundred yards away. The cannon mechanism recoiled, the empty brass shell case came out, the tank rocked slightly on its suspension system, and the fire mission ended. At the completion we had a substantial pile of empty 90m/m brass cases on the left side of each tank that had been thrown out of the loader's hatch.

The five crews were in the process of policing up the two firing sites when Captain Barrett showed up. He arrived unannounced because we did not have anyone at the foot of the hill to call ahead and alert the top of the hill of a visitor. Barrett had taken command of Charlie Company about two months earlier, having just left a tank unit with the 7th U.S. Army, Germany. He was strong on the cavalry traditions inherited by armor, and our current static warfare rubbed his philosophy the wrong way. Regardless, he had made his way to Korea because, as he stated, "It may be ugly, but it's the only war we've got." His visit fell into the normal pattern of concern for what was going on with his troops. It gave him the opportunity to see, feel, smell, and hear what was happening at the cutting edge of combat and personally assess how his troops were doing. My platoon, under the operational control of the 2nd Battalion, 7th Infantry Regiment, had removed Barrett from direct responsibility for the actions of my platoon. It was my view that he was here today to reassure himself that the 2nd Battalion was employing me properly. I briefed him on our situation: mission, communications, command responsibilities in working with the 2nd Battalion, logistic support, and current gunnery exercises. He inspected our two tank positions. On exiting the "21" tank crew bunker, he stated, "Jack, this is a terrible way to deploy armor! The name of the game is shock action, and here you sit on top of a hill taking pot shots at Chinks."

I did not respond. He was not criticizing me personally. This was a way to let off steam for circumstances beyond his control.

"Have you ever been quartered in a bunker before? Everybody up here is in bunkers except your three tanks at the foot of the hill."

"No, this is new," I said. "The only adjustment to living in a bunker has been learning to deal with the rats. They're everywhere." Barrett gave a sympathetic shake of his head.

Barrett concluded, "One more thing. I spoke with the 2nd Battalion S-3 before I came up here. He indicated you'd be relieved in two more days. Did you know that?"

"No, sir, I didn't," I replied. "I talked to him just this morning to get firing clearance, and he said nothing about the relief."

"No matter," Barrett said. "It was probably brand-new information when I got there a little while ago. Check with him for details. I'm heading back to Charlie Company now. Oh, the mail is here in the quarter-ton." He handed me the packet. "Good luck!" His vehicle left a dusty trail as he departed down the hill.

Well, I thought, that was that! One more day of gunnery and then disengage for a dusty road march back to showers and hot chow.

It was around 2230 hours when a mortar barrage hit Hill 199. I had returned to the "21" bunker from inspecting the guard for the "22" tank and was about to call Holt for his guard schedule for the tank perimeter.

Suddenly, deafening explosions erupted all around us. The interior of the bunker was lit up as bright, strobelike flashes of light found their way around the sandbagged entrance and through our small ventilation window. Concussion waves struck the bunker in rapid succession; the ground shook. Surprise, confusion, and terror put me in a state of paralysis. An urge to run was neutralized by an urge to crawl into a hole. I was frozen stiff with fear. In a half-crouched position, I felt my knees going weak. What was happening? I wondered. How do I protect myself? I did not realize, at that moment, that we were in a mortar attack. From wondering where to find a hole to crawl into, my thoughts shifted to wondering whether our bunker could withstand a direct hit. I had never experienced this type of situation before.

There had been no warning of incoming rounds. With mortars all you hear just prior to detonation is the wind softly whistling through the mortar tail fins. And you had to be very close to the incoming round to hear it. It was a very different sound from that of artillery. Incoming artillery gave a second or two of warning. The rounds came in with a kind of sucking sound coupled with an overtone that gave a "whoosh—whoosh—whoosh" effect. I was learning something new with these Chinese 120m/m mortars. The barrage ended as abruptly as it had started; it probably did not last a minute. How many rounds had landed? Where? With the ground and bunker shaking, the brilliant light flashing, and the roar of the explosions sounding, I guessed that they landed right outside the bunker entrance.

Every face in the bunker had a stunned, terrified look—including me, I am sure. As the new quiet settled in I asked, "Anyone hurt? Is everyone O.K?" Satisfied that everyone was all right, I exited the bunker cautiously and approached the "21" tank. Sergeant Gardner was on guard duty in the tank. My eyes adjusted to the dark, and I could see the tank was completely buttoned-up—all the hatches were closed. I shouted for Gardner but got no response. With a rock I banged on the turret, and soon the tank commander's hatch opened, and Gardner's head came into view.

"Gardner, are you all right?" I asked.

"Yes, sir, I'm O.K. Was all that meant for us?"

"I don't know," I answered. "We'll wait until morning and take a look around to see how close they came."

I walked over to the "22" tank; they were all right. Then I went over to the Heavy Mortar Company CP. The CO was very agitated—really jumpy. He said this was the first mortar attack on Hill 199 in about a week. We had received an estimated twenty rounds. He had not received any reports of casualties or damage. Returned mortar fire was not planned because our counterbattery radar, a new and relatively untried system, had not acquired a fix on the incoming rounds. The radar could locate the position from which the mortar rounds originated with a high level of precision, but it had to catch the rounds while they were in flight. In effect, counterbattery radar would re-create the trajectory and calculate the path back from the point of impact to the point of origin.

"Who are they shooting at, you or me?" I asked.

"I don't know. I've been here awhile, and you've just arrived. I will say it's been relatively quiet until you got here. You're visible here on the hilltop, you're active, and you may be hurting them. And they know exactly where you are. You know the story—tanks attract attention!"

As I walked back to the "21" bunker, I tried to put events into perspective. The mortar attack had been scary because you can do nothing about it except sit there and take it. An event like that cannot be objectively and rationally dismissed as a random occurrence, like a lightening strike. No, a mortar attack had to be treated subjectively. And, in all honesty, I had just been frightened to my innermost core. This was not the first time I had been through a review of my mortality since arriving in Korea. Fear of death is a normal instinct. In combat this fear becomes exponentially magnified because the enemy is actively trying to kill you. Intensified, fear of death assumes a larger-than-normal proportion of your thought processes—both awake and asleep. This preoccupation, in some cases, can totally disable a person—inhibit his ability to function mentally and physically. It is called battle fatigue (shell shock). The mortar attack tonight had brought me, again, to the question: "How am I doing?" The answer did not require a very sophisticated rationalization. I was doing fine. The fact that I was able to examine my situation demonstrated my control over circumstances. If ever I did succumb to battle fatigue, I reasoned, I would be so devastated psychologically that I would be incapable of even asking the question about how I was doing. All right, I thought, let me put this episode behind me and get on with platoon leading. Vulnerability to the mortar attack and safety were my immediate concern. My main thought was of the five tank crews. What more could be done to improve their safety? Nothing came to mind. We tankers were on common ground with the infantry—our exposure to the hazard was shared equally. Like the infantry, our response to the mortar attack had been to hunker down and endure the incoming rounds—and pray the bunker would not get a direct hit. The tank crews had a measurable advantage—we would be out of here the day after tomorrow. Our expected exposure was short term compared to the infantry; they would be on the MLR for months. I tried to reckon the toll, the psychological cost, that the mortar attacks took on an individual over an extended period of time. Without a measuring stick I had only my own reaction to the attack tonight as a guide. My best assessment was that nobody was going to come off the MLR unscathed. The longer the duration of exposure, the deeper would be the mental scars.

At the bunker I was told that Holt had called to find out what was going on. I returned the call, repeated the viewpoint of the Heavy Weapons Company CO, and inquired how close the barrage had come to the tank perimeter. Holt stated that the barrage had landed a long way from the perimeter, to the east. We agreed to meet at the hilltop in the morning to plan activities for our last day up front and concluded our conversation.

It had been a long day, but sleep did not come effortlessly. I wrestled with the mortar attack for some time and knew I would not easily put this episode behind me. The phrase "Tanks attract attention" kept repeating itself in my head.

Fourth Day, 0800 Hours

With morning, we examined our hilltop for the effects of last night's barrage. We did not find any craters anywhere near the tank positions. We did find some halfway down the rear slope of the hill. If those mortar rounds were meant for the tanks, they missed the mark by a long way.

This is easy to do when trying to hit a ridgeline with a high-trajectory weapon such as a mortar. Artillery and mortars are relatively inaccurate; they are designed to strike a small zone rather than a pinpoint position. The longer the range to the target, the greater is the dispersion of the strike of the rounds. Artillerymen know this fact well, and they compensate for inaccuracy by firing many rounds at a target. They saturate the target area. Salvos and barrages are fired with the sure knowledge that statistics are on their side—out of many rounds one or more are likely to land precisely on the target. In our case, the tanks sat on a knifelike ridge with steep slopes in front and back. A miss in this event was as good as a mile. To reduce the visibility and attractiveness of the tanks as a target, I had both of them covered with camouflage netting. Anyway, I thought, the plan was to be off this hill tomorrow.

Plans and intentions formed at the start of a day can be totally transformed before the day is over. Early in March 1952, I experienced that kind of a day, one filled with twists and turns that ended with a totally unpredictable outcome. I was the leader of a reconnaissance team from Charlie Company to assess an area beyond the MLR related to a 15th Infantry Regiment counterattack plan. The contingency plan included a company of tanks to provide direct-fire support for the infantry. Two days prior to this, the Chinese had made a battalion-strength probe in this sector of the MLR. Anticipating another assault, we designed the counterattack plan to be as punishing as possible. A company of tanks, included in the plan, would be capable of delivering devastating direct-fire support. Our reconnaissance party consisted of myself and eight noncommissioned officers (NCOs). The NCOs were all tank commanders, representing the four platoons of Charlie Company. The size and composition of our group had been dictated by the possibility of the counterattack plan being initiated during the hours of darkness. We needed a good proportion of our troop leaders to have a familiarity with the terrain in which we would be maneuvering. Our reconnaissance would determine the feasibility of the terrain to permit a tank-infantry counterattack. I sought out the infantry company commander responsible for this sector of the MLR and explained my mission. He stated that he was not aware of any enemy activity to his immediate front that day. He knew of no enemy or friendly minefields.

The MLR was situated on a low ridgeline that faced a high ridgeline occupied by the Chinese. Between the ridges was a mile-wide valley of relatively flat terrain. No dwellings existed in the valley, and the surface appeared to be a series of low folds in the earth running parallel to the ridges. Our ridgeline had a gap in it that was about a half-mile wide that gave access to the valley. A trail went through the gap and followed a small meandering creek toward the enemy lines. The gap appeared to have all the requirements of an entrance for tanks into the valley, and the valley looked to be well suited for a tank-infantry attack. The creek presented a question mark. Were the banks of the creek steep enough to be an obstacle to tank movement?

The mid-morning sun had taken off some of the sharp winter chill. It was a calm, cloudless day. Lightly armed, our party advanced on foot along the snow-covered trail and into the valley. All along the way we saw evidence of the fighting that had occurred several days earlier. The field was littered with the incidental debris and trash of combat. Among the items we saw were articles of clothing, "C" rations (combat rations) both eaten and uneaten, empty cloth bandoleers, empty ammunition boxes, water cans, spools of telephone wire, paper trash, piles of empty brass cartridge cases sitting above the snow where a machine gun had been fired, and pockmarked earth in black contrast with the snow where mortar and artillery shells had hit. Our group stopped on a roll of ground at the forward edge of the U.S. counterattack two days earlier. We were about three hundred yards in front of the MLR. Everyone agreed that the terrain was well suited to tank maneuvers and that the creek banks presented no obstacle. Our reconnaissance was completed.

Crack! Crack! Crack! Three loud, piercing reports snapped close to our heads. Someone shouted, "Take cover!" We all dropped to the ground. We heard more sharp reports just over our heads: it was small-arms fire. Instinctively, I pushed backward to put the mound of the terrain between the source of fire and myself. The report of the enemy gun was muffled, indicating it was a long distance away, probably more than three hundred yards. Quickly, the crack of bullets overhead turned to very closely spaced reports—automatic fire. I shouted: "Anybody hit?" No one had been injured.

Face down on the lightly snow-covered ground, I glanced about and thought of the situation we were in. We were armed with pistols, and the closest support was three hundred yards to our rear. Moreover, the enemy had our range; bullets were now striking the top of the mound we were hiding behind and throwing showers of frozen dirt. The predicament we were in did not conform to the plan with which I had started the day. Moments ago I had been fat, dumb, and happy, and now I was face down in the snow and had become the target for Chinese gunners. Lying there I became conscious of an acrid odor that I could not identify. What was that smell? I then noticed that I was lying in what appeared to be a hazy, thin, bluish-gray fog. Looking to both sides I found this fog was like a blanket about two feet thick. It extended many yards in each direction from me. Other, more immediate and important events were taking place, and I dismissed the fog phenomenon. I concentrated on the fix we were in and how the team would extricate itself. My orders were to infiltrate back to the MLR singly and to keep low to avoid attracting attention. We were to crawl on our bellies for the first hundred yards, using the mound we were behind to shield us from observation by the Chinese. We waited for about ten minutes after the firing stopped and then began our stealthy withdrawal to the MLR. The return to the MLR was time consuming but without incident, and everyone was relieved to have successfully handled a serious situation. Later in the day, however, before evening chow call, matters took a different turn.

Six of the tank commanders complained of being ill. The symptoms were a severe headache, a queasy stomach, and a burning sensation in bloodshot eyes. The other two tank commanders and I had none of these symptoms. Everyone in the reconnaissance party, however, was conscious of the unusual bluish-gray haze that surrounded us as we took cover from the Chinese small-arms fire. Possibly the fog phenomenon had something to do with the physical condition that was common to six personnel in our party. Having six out of nine personnel come down ill the same day with identical symptoms seemed beyond coincidence. A call was made to headquarters, 64th Tank Battalion, and after we explained the situation, the battalion surgeon directed that our reconnaissance group, all nine of us, report immediately to him. Our surgeon was very thorough in his medical examination of all of us. He recorded the symptoms, and with the S-2 (Intelligence officer) present, he obtained a detailed description from each of us concerning the bluish-gray fog. We were all treated with an ointment for our eyes whether we needed it or not. At this point I was becoming concerned about what I had been exposed to beyond the MLR. My day had taken another unplanned turn. Although none of our party showed life-threatening signs, the surgeon was concerned about the baffling medical condition. The battalion S-2 was now involved and was talking rather ominously with the surgeon about Chinese dirty tricks—such as chemical and biological warfare. The acronym CBR (chemical-biological-radiological) came up repeatedly as the surgeon and S-2 conversed. The dialog was not lost on the members of our reconnaissance party. This was serious business. Accordingly, a call was made to headquarters, 3rd Infantry Division, and the episode, with emphasis on the bluish-gray fog, was explained. Someone at the 3rd Infantry Division quickly decided to pursue this matter with all possible haste. This is a quick reaction, I thought. It appeared that division found the prospect of Chinese CBR warfare tactics a credible possibility. The situation was getting more serious by the minute. Arrangements were made for the division chemical officer to be escorted to the site of the fog the following morning. I was selected to be the escort officer. Although I felt well enough, the possibility of having been exposed to some incipient health condition could not easily be ignored. Going back to the fog site was low on my roster of things I wanted to do. Whatever my plan had been at the beginning of the day, it was now totally unrecognizable. Two NCOs from the S-2 section were also selected to make up the escort party.

The division chemical officer, a captain, arrived at headquarters, 64th Tank Battalion, at 0900 hours. Both the battalion surgeon and the S-2 briefed him. As we drove to what was now called the CBR site, I filled him in on what I had observed the previous day. He indicated that the 15th Infantry Regiment staff had been alerted to the incident and were aware of the coming inspection of the site. At this stage the simple terrain reconnaissance of yesterday had ballooned into the possibility of a major event with the potential of international complications.

During the short ride to the site, the chemical officer volunteered the information that he had never been forward of the MLR and that he was a bit apprehensive about the mission we were on. I assured him that I was anxious myself, having been under fire the previous day. As I thought about it, those three hundred yards beyond the MLR seemed like a very long distance. We parked behind the MLR ridge, near the gap. Again, I sought out the company commander of this sector and asked whether he knew of any enemy patrols or activity in front of the MLR. To his knowledge nothing was going on.

Again, it was mid-morning and sunny, cold, and calm as our party of four advanced in twenty-yard intervals to the CBR site. As we approached the area we readily saw the bluish-gray blanket of fog. I observed no change from what I had seen yesterday; the strong acrid smell permeated the air. The blanket lay a foot or two above the earth. I found myself hesitating to step into the fog. CBR, and its implications, had become part of my vocabulary. Our party crouched behind the fold in the terrain to avoid attracting the attention of the Chinese. I looked to the chemical officer for some confirmation of the import of the hazy, bluish-gray fog. He had been intently studying the ground. Eventually, he looked relieved and then smiled widely.

"Lieutenant," he said, "the CBR scare is over. Hell, all we're dealing with is white phosphorous. It smells like WP, and if you look at the ground closely, you'll see small puffs of smoke erupting, causing the fog." He let out a laugh, and the two NCOs and I, in a nervous response, laughed with him. Could it be that simple? Were we dealing with a nonevent? His self-assured manner told us that it was, indeed, just WP.

He was certainly right about the puffs of smoke. Staring at the ground, we would see a puff of smoke emerge from time to time. The explanation of the low-lying fog was rudimentary once the mechanism was understood. During the fighting several days ago, WP shells or grenades had been detonated in this area. Small fragments of the white phosphorous had become embedded in the frozen surface of the earth and became insulated from the air. Although this day, as the other day, was cold, and in spite of the light snow cover, the bright sun thawed the earth, which permitted air to reach the fragments. The result was a small puff of smoke as the WP burned. The calm, windless air permitted the puffs to accumulate into a foggy blanket at the base of the fold in the terrain. Conditions had to be favorable for this phenomenon to occur. Without sun, the fragments would remain embedded in the earth, shielded from the air. A slight wind would readily dissipate the puff of smoke, and the foggy blanket would not form. The captain directed that each of us, using empty C ration cans, gather samples of earth from where a puff of smoke occurred. He said the samples would be tested back at division to confirm his field inspection conclusion. In short order all four of us had a can in each hand and began our walk back to the MLR. I had a sense of gratification that I had not been subjected to a real CBR event. My sense of well being, however, was soon to be disrupted.

Boom! One hundred yards to our right, in the open valley, an artillery shell came crashing in. The Chinese had our range. The choice was to duck for whatever cover we could find or to run. I shouted, "Run!" Before the next round came in I had a fleeting moment to wonder what was in the minds of the Chinese. Did four people represent a worthy artillery target? The second round had the same shrill incoming sound as the first. The round landed in about the same place as the first, but it was just a single round, not a salvo. We kept running, but by this time it was more like a staggering trot. You cannot run for an extended distance in winter clothing when wearing winter-issue insulated Mickey Mouse boots. The Chinese artillery rounds kept pace with our lumbering retreat, but they all kept landing one hundred yards to our right. All told, the Chinese fired six rounds but never made an azimuth correction. We must have been a sight to see, clutching our C ration cans and hustling toward the MLR to the cadence of enemy artillery. We got a good-hearted hoot and a holler from the 15th Infantry riflemen as our breathless party found the safety of the MLR. Riflemen got shot at on a daily basis; it was part of their environment. It was diverting, for a change, to watch someone else cope with enemy fire. Later, I tried to rationalize the intentions of the Chinese artillerymen firing single rounds one hundred yards off-line with the target, but the episode defied reasoned speculation.

Back at the 64th Tank Battalion the chemical officer briefed the battalion staff and then returned to headquarters, 3rd Infantry Division, with his C ration can samples. He also took with him a war story about a CBR scare beyond the MLR and how he solved the affair and survived enemy fire.

A puzzle remained that was never resolved to anyone's satisfaction. How do you explain the six crewmen with splitting headaches, bloodshot and burning eyes, and queasy stomachs? What was the common denominator of that medical problem?

For me, the two days of the CBR scare brought home the concept of being prepared to make continuing adjustments to your plans. Do not get too fixed on your plan for the day—it could be drastically changed before day's end.

My plan on this next to the last day on Hill 199 had been to conduct gunnery practice. Instead, I elected to get an early start on preparations for moving out. Both crews on the hill busied themselves with the details of the coming motor march and breaking camp. They paid particular attention to leaving a well-policed area. By early afternoon the two crews on top of the hill had gone about as far as they could in preparation for the next day's move. All that remained was to close the latrines and load up the bedding in the morning. I had not received any instructions from the S-3, so I decided to go see him and touch base with Holt while I was down there. Davis and I drove down to the perimeter.

I could see that the three crews were ready for the march. I could also see that Holt had a somber expression on his face.

"What's up?" I asked.

"Sir, I don't think you're going to like this—those tanks from the 7th Tank Company aren't coming tomorrow." He paused to let that soak in and finished with, "I heard it through the rumor mill."

"What!" I knew Holt wasn't joking, but I was having a hard time swallowing this news.

"The word is that Ordnance is waiting for repair parts. There were more things wrong with those tanks than just the transmission."

"Since when?" I asked. I did not really expect Holt to know the answer to that.

"I don't know," he replied. "I figured you wouldn't be too happy with this news coming at this late date. I just found out a few minutes ago."

In the few days we had been here, Holt had developed his own private information network. It was out of normal channels, but it worked. I was quite sure he had the facts right.

"O.K." I said, "I'm on my way to see the S-3 and find out how official this is." As I left I turned and said, "Same old story. Five percent never get the word."

The Operations bunker smelled of new construction. I had to wait until the S-3 finished a conversation on the field telephone.

"How do you like our new quarters?" Captain Hornstein asked.

"Yeah, nice quarters," I said quickly. I wanted to get right to the subject uppermost on my mind. "Captain, I just heard that there is a problem about my platoon being relieved tomorrow. Did I hear correctly? You know, I'm all packed and ready to go. I've got five tank crews that are all set to move out."

"Sit down," he responded. "How did you get word of this so fast? I just found out myself twenty minutes ago. In fact, I called your bunker, but they said you had left and were on your way here. Word sure gets around fast." He then developed the same story that had been told by Holt, except in more detail.

"What's the new plan?" I asked. "I'm going to have to get in touch with my company commander."

"All I can tell you is that the repairs will take a few more days," he said. "I can't be more definite than that. You're right, you better call your CO—he may already know something about this change in plans."

Change in plans! I'll say it's a change in plans, I thought to myself. I have been through changes in plans and diminished expectations ever since I started on this mission. A "few more days" could mean anything. How complicated were the new repairs? Were repair parts on hand? That and a half dozen more questions went through my mind. I have sure been doing a lot of adjusting to change in the last few days, I thought.

I went to the Headquarters Company communications bunker to call directly from their switchboard. The fewer switchboards and wire you went through, the stronger the signal would be between phones. My call went to "Killer Switch" (3rd Infantry Division Signal Company) at division headquarters, who put me through to "Sprocket Switch" (64th Tank Battalion), who put me through to "Sprocket Forward" (Charlie Company). The call had to go through miles and miles of field telephone wire, with the signal losing strength every mile. The signal between me and Barrett was weak. I was lucky to get through and luckier still to catch him at the Charlie Company CP. Barrett heard me out. He was not aware of the change in plans, but he was philosophical about accepting the inevitable. He said he would get right on the problem and get back to me as promptly as he could get answers. Meanwhile, I was to continue my mission with the 2nd Battalion, 7th Infantry Regiment, as initially assigned.

By the time I got back to the Operations bunker, I had reconciled myself to this change in plans. I advised the S-3 of my conversation with Barrett and concluded with, "Do you have any new targets for me?"

The tank crews showed little concern one way or the other regarding the change in plans. Actually, being attached to the 2nd Battalion was relatively light duty. No fatigue details were placed on the platoon. We were here to support the infantry mission, which at present was to hold the line. In this defensive role, just being on hand, in place, was all that was expected of the platoon. We received no fire missions to support infantry action; the gunnery, which was aggressive, was my idea, and it was designed to promote crew cross training and keep the men on their toes. And the Chinese were quiet, if you discounted their patrolling activity and the occasional mortar barrage. The mortar attacks occurred usually at night. The Chinese did not dare fire during daylight hours for fear of being spotted by fixed-wing aircraft with artillery observers on board. Once spotted, they would find that our counterbattery fire on their position was overwhelming. The Chinese used their artillery very sparingly even at night; mortars seemed to be their main weapon. Up on the hill we moved back into our bunkers, and at the perimeter Sergeant First Class Holt and the three tank crews resumed the same activities as the previous three days.

Fourth Day, 1630 Hours

No new targets, real or "suspected," had been supplied by the S-3, so I decided to hold off on the gunnery for the next several days. The platoon would be kept busy with gun and vehicle maintenance and housekeeping improvement. My concern was maintaining morale, discipline, and an aggressive spirit. Sitting inert in the Korean summer, with few amusements and a mission that bordered on being totally dormant, presented a leadership challenge. Improving our housekeeping situation had been put on the back burner because of our initially planned short stay. Now that the stay had been extended, it was time to increase our home comforts. We dug new latrines. At the foot of the hill we made the slit trenches larger and deeper. We erected clotheslines so the bedding could be aired out during the day. We also applied more sandbags to the bunker (figure 3). At the top of the hill, parking for the quarter-ton had been a problem. We needed a permanent solution to permit traffic to use the road without being blocked by the vehicle. When the tank was not in the revetment, it was down the slope in full defilade and occupied the place normally used by the quarter-ton. There was no room, then, to park the quarter-ton except in the road. We would need to rebuild the existing collapsed parking spot. I assigned the "garage" project to Sergeant Gardner and outlined my task instructions in general terms: he could use our bunker construction as a building guide; he could use the timbers at the "22" tank position for the frame; he could use tank on-vehicle material (OVM) tools; he could rely on Headquarters Company, 2nd Battalion, for bunker material such as sandbags; and he could avail himself of ten men from the platoon as needed. I wanted the "garage" completed in two days. Gardner received his orders late in the afternoon of our fourth day. I called Holt and instructed him to provide six men for the work detail as needed; the remaining four would come from the "21" and "22" tanks.

This project, a group effort, gave me the opportunity to observe Gardner's organizational and leadership skills. More than that, I could evaluate the teamwork potential of two new members to the "21" tank. The Korean service time rotation system kept personnel moving in and out of the platoon constantly. This turnover presented a continuing crew training challenge.

My new loader was an African American. He was tall and had a strong build. He represented the initial influx of personnel to fulfill President Harry Truman's order for the integration of the U.S. forces.[5] In a sense, he became the focal point of this social engineering dynamic for the 2nd Platoon. As such he was a pioneer—which is pretty much the way he approached his new role as a U.S. soldier in a new kind of world. He was feeling his way, as were we all. His interrelationship with other

Figure 3. Home improvement. Entrance is at the left. Note the small ventilation window.

members of the platoon, his acceptance, would hinge primarily on his performance as a competent crewman. It was obvious he had absorbed and retained, and brought with him, a lot of his basic training from Fort Knox, the Armored Training Center. He was a quiet, attentive listener, and you knew he was making a special effort to perform his assigned tasks in a manner to leave no room for criticism. President Truman's integration order was not going to falter for lack of application on his part. He was uncomplaining and a hard worker, and my expectation was that he would make a first-class tanker.

Proximity to combat provided the incentive to be really good at your assigned job. Members of the platoon applied themselves to learning their role as tank crewmen with sincere interest. There is nothing like getting shot at to alter your attitude toward training. The closer one came to the front line, the more positive was the effect on attentiveness and application to schooling. The other new crew member, the "21" tank's new bow gunner, fit the role of an interested and involved student. I had placed him in the least-demanding position of a crewman—bow gunner. I expected that he would adjust to the cross training quickly and

Figure 4. Home away from home. The quarter-ton truck was backed into the "garage" for protection. Empty ammunition boxes are stacked to the right of the bunker. The "21" tank is in full defilade at left.

become a real asset. He was deliberate in everything he did, however; "quick" or "brisk" was not part of his vocabulary. It was not that he did not make the effort or try—he did. He was a conscientious and willing learner, but the pace left something to be desired. I was sure that once he became familiar with the routine of his duties and had experience working with the crew, his confidence would be reinforced and his pace would pick up.

SIXTH AND SEVENTH DAYS

The "garage" project, under Gardner's supervision, turned out to be a first-rate structure. It was completed on our sixth day (figure 4).

As the days wore on with no word of our relief, I was becoming more and more conscious of a need to keep the platoon involved in constructive activities. I had Holt work up a schedule for the men to bathe and swim in the Imjin River. A river ford was located about one-half mile

Figure 5. Looking south toward Hill 199 toward main supply route; camouflage road cannot be seen. Hill 355 is the high point on the horizon. Valley at left center leads to Imjin River.

down a trail to the east of Holt's position; the ford could be seen from my position on Hill 199. No more than two men were allowed to be away from a five-man tank crew at any one time. The quarter-ton was used for transport, and everyone had a turn roughly every other day. I reported this diversion as field sanitation. If the Imjin was polluted, it never had an effect on any of us (figures 5 and 6). Tanks need a lot of maintenance, so keeping busy was easy to do. All crews, both on top of the hill and at the foot in the perimeter, had daily routines to follow in the upkeep of the tanks. Emphasis was on crew cross training. The activities included cleaning the gun tubes; attending to numerous oil and lubrication fittings; checking and maintaining fluid levels; checking track; replacing faulty end connectors; servicing small arms, including the machine guns; and resupplying ammunition (figure 7).

A person does not enjoy much privacy in a bunker shared with five other people. At the end of the day, after the normal duties had been attended to, we had a leisure period before turning in for a night's rest. The crew talked a lot—endlessly. I could not help but hear the conver-

Figure 6. Imjin River from Hill 199, looking southeast. River ford is where the valley meets the river. "Playground" area is to the left center of photo on east bank of the river.

sations, and I admired the variety of subject matter. They joked and kidded with each other, and sometimes I would find myself in their conversation. This was a brotherhood, an exclusive fraternity of "those who have been shot at." Within the entire 3rd Infantry Division, which was about fifteen thousand men, only a small percentage, about three thousand, was on the MLR in contact with the enemy. To the rear were the rest of the division, then I Corps, and then the 8th Army rear. Behind every man on the line, there were about eight men in a support role. If you have ever been shot at, you know you are a member of a very select group. Euphemistically, this group is called the "cutting edge." The main topic of conversation was women—well, girls actually. Young men eighteen to twenty years of age have a keen interest in females. And here, up front, we lived in a sterile world devoid of females. So, the small talk was heavily laced with fantasy, vulgarity, reverie, expectation, and hope, hope that they would live to see their expectations, however great or small, triumph. The nearest opportunity for any form of triumph was via R&R leave in Japan. Leave is permission for absence from duty—a va-

Figure 7. Resupply of ammunition. The "21" tank is in defilade, out of sight to the enemy. Ammunition is being inspected for damage before being stowed in the tank.

cation. The delights and joy of five days' leave in Japan had been circulated, and amplified, by those who had been there. The stories were a mingling of embroidered facts and fantasy. As one can well imagine, in a broad range of priorities, R&R was high on the list of topics discussed. And it was discussed, over and over again.

EIGHTH AND NINTH DAYS

On our eighth day up front, Holt called to state that I had visitors coming up the hill. First Lieutenant Stanley J. Joltan and First Lieutenant Gustov C. Hinrich, Charlie Company, on a route reconnaissance, had extended the scope of their mission to include Hill 199. Stan led the 4th Platoon, and Gus commanded the 1st Platoon.

The two of them, dust covered, were a welcome sight. I showed them around the top of the hill: our revetments and bunkers, the Heavy Mortar Company area, and the terrain of scenic interest held by the Chinese. The bunkers were a novelty to them, and they admired the "garage." In turn, they brought me up to date on what was happening in Charlie Company and the 64th Tank Battalion—which was not much. Activity had slowed down all along the front held by the 3rd Division. This information tallied with my local situation. Apparently the goal now was to avoid rocking the boat while the truce talks at Panmunjom seemed to be seriously progressing to a conclusion. More to the point, Captain Barrett had been working with our battalion to get the 703rd Ordnance Company to hasten the repair and release of the tanks of the 7th Tank Company. Although Gus did not know the details of the repairs, he said that the location of the repair parts, that is, whether they were in Korea or in Japan, could dictate the length of time for the repair work. He added that possibly the tanks could be evacuated to the rear for third-echelon maintenance. The 703rd had not volunteered a completion date.

"Don't worry, Jack," Stan said. "Every day you're on this hill you establish a new record in the battalion. No platoon has ever been on detached duty this long."

"Stan," I chuckled, "I didn't come up here to break any records—believe me!" I added, "Except for the gunnery, and swimming in the Imjin, and getting mortars dumped on us once in awhile, this is pretty dull duty for a tank platoon."

As they motored down the hill, I gave them a half-envious wave. Their visit had been a refreshing interlude in a daily lifestyle that was becoming a heavy grind—it was a dull routine. Sitting on this sun-baked ridgeline day after day had exhausted the novelty of being on the front line. It was the same for the tanks in the perimeter at the foot of the hill. Our daily routine had an unremarkable sameness to earlier days. The activities conducted today were a mirror of the previous day. We were locked in a never-changing world. And it was a world without current, up-to-date news. We had no daily newspapers, and the personal portable commercial-band radios produced little but music, at best. The lack of information of the world beyond our MLR position amplified the dullness of our activities. Chinese H&I, unwelcome as it was, provided the only stimulus of the day. As a troop leader, I was conscious that a major goal was combating complacency in my tankers. As the days blended into each other, I knew that the gunnery exercises would have to be reinforced with some other activity to maintain a cutting-edge fighting spirit. At the moment I was at a loss as to what form that activity would take.

Tenth Day, 1100 Hours

The morning gunnery exercise on "suspected" targets had just ceased on our tenth day when Holt called to alert me to another visitor. Major Thompson L. Raney, executive officer, 64th Tank Battalion, was on his way up the hill. What is this all about? I wondered. A visit from battalion staff was clearly out of the ordinary. I quickly glanced around the "21" area. Except for the pile of empty brass shell cases, the position looked presentable. I stepped down to the road to await the arrival of Major Raney.

I saluted, greeted him, and directed his driver to pull up and park behind the "21" tank, which was still in the revetment. Major Raney informed me that our battalion CO, Lieutenant Colonel Emerson W. Grant, wanted a firsthand report on the activities of the 2nd Platoon, Charlie Company. He added that out of the entire battalion, my platoon was the only element directly engaged with the enemy.

"Major Raney, I'll be very pleased to show you around." I was relieved to know that the basis for his visit was strictly to gather information. "You just missed our fire mission for this morning. The 2nd Battalion S-3 provides me with targets, and the platoon works them over with HE, sometimes WP."

"I heard your guns when I came down the camouflage section of the MSR." He paused, looking toward Hill 317, and said, "Show me what you were shooting at."

We stood next to the "21" tank, and using my marked-up topographical map with the grid squares, I showed him the targets we had engaged.

"The targets are only 'suspected,'" I said. I reached into the tank and got my ten-power binoculars and handed them to the major. "Take a look at the one that is on the ridge beyond Outpost Tessie, about eighteen hundred yards. It's on the left side of the saddle in the ridge. To be honest, I really don't know if that is a man-made structure or what. The intelligence that the S-3 had is that it was an aperture of a bunker. A reconnaissance patrol brought in the information. It took one ranging shot to get the yardage right, and then we put two HE on it for effect. What do you think?"

He studied the target for about a minute, making minor focusing adjustments, and said, "Hell, I don't know—could be legitimate. Whatever it was, your HE has it all torn up. Any problems with ammunition resupply? If the logistic stream is slow, I'd think twice before firing at targets as indeterminate as that one."

"No, sir, no problem," I said with emphasis. "I call in my requirements to the S-4 in the afternoon, and the morning chow truck drops off the rounds. The ammunition wells in all the tanks are full up. We never use the stowed rounds. I'll tell you one thing, sir: when I come off this hill, I'll have the best gunners in the battalion."

"I'll bet you will," he replied with a smile. "I had a chat with Major Crain before I came up here. He said your crews are shooting targets just about every day."

"That's about right. I rotate the crews. These two tanks up here serve as firing platforms for the whole platoon."

We talked at length about the fields of fire available to me. We then talked about the subject of logistics. I told him I could find no fault with the way the 2nd Battalion handled supply to Hill 199 for both the tanks and the Heavy Mortar Company. Everyone on the hill was satisfied with the supplies and ammunition delivery. I noted that Sergeant Holt and the three crews at the foot of the hill ate with Headquarters Company. The food prepared by that mess sergeant, serving the battalion staff, was first-rate. We ate the same food, but it was a little cooler by the time it was delivered from a marmite can. Major Raney was particularly interested in troop morale.

"Jack, how long has your platoon been up front? I know it's longer than anyone at battalion can remember for a detached unit. What's your view of the morale of your tankers?"

"Morale is excellent, sir. We've been here ten days, and we'll probably be able to leave in a few more. In a sense, we're isolated from the normal environment of being with Charlie Company and surrounded by tank company routine and activities. It's a cinch we don't have any movies up here on the hill. But we're in the midst of a battalion of infantry, so we're not actually alone. There is plenty to do to keep busy, but it's the same routine every day—and that is starting to wear thin. No variety except for getting shot at on an unscheduled basis. When the Chinks send in the mortar rounds, they send a lot of them, about every other night. It's H&I, and everyone gets it—on the hill, at the bottom of the hill, and up and down along the MLR. To tell the truth, I think getting shot at has put a lot of motivation into our gunnery exercises. The chow is good, and it is served regularly, the medical aid station is within walking distance, and church call is equally close. Up front here we're getting four-point time for rotation purposes, which suits everybody. There are no discipline problems. The men respond to orders promptly and willingly. My view is that morale is excellent. Would you like to talk to my troopers?"

He stated he did not think that was necessary but that he would like to see the rest of the hilltop. He examined the "21" bunker briefly and said, "Looks substantial enough. Between this bunker and the revetment, you walked into a nice setup. Any idea of how long the 7th Infantry has been here to install these improvements?"

"Sir, I don't know how long they have been on the line in this location. The 7th was holding this area last November during the fight for Little Gibraltar. In fact, my platoon was in a blocking position at the ford down there." I pointed to the south toward the Imjin River, the place we were currently using for bathing. "I think that the 7th Regiment had a break sometime after that before returning here."

"I'm starting to get my bearings," he replied. "Isn't that the 'Playground' over there?" His gaze shifted farther to the south and east, beyond the ford, and followed the river, which swept in a gentle curve southward. The terrain on the east bank was wide, flat, and sandy, which merged inland with low rolling hills. This area was behind our lines, and tanks could easily maneuver in the hills; the river bank was like a superhighway—miles and miles of relatively flat terrain. The 64th Tank Battalion had adopted it as a training ground the previous winter.

"Was it March or April when the whole battalion participated in the attack exercise?" he asked.

"It was March, sir. A damn cold day."

"Yes. Your platoon was the aggressor force and provided the delaying action. That was a good exercise." He smiled, recalling the day.

"I had over a week, off and on, to study the terrain. On the map it looks pretty flat, but when you're walking the ground, a lot of choke points can be found. I learned a lot about slowing down a battalion in the attack. It's a nervous proposition when you have sixty-seven tanks coming at you."

"Well, it was a busy day with useful lessons learned. What's that area beyond the 'Two-Two' tank?" He was looking at the Heavy Mortar Company location.

We went to the "22" tank first. Major Raney was interested in the field of fire available from that position. Then we went to the Heavy Mortar Company CP. I introduced Major Raney to the CO, who briefly described his mission and explained they were developing mortar concentrations in front of the MLR. As we left, a salvo of the mortars was fired, and the sharp cough of the 4.2-inch tubes followed us down the road.

We returned to where his quarter-ton was parked, and he said, "Jack, you've got your mission well in hand here. Shall I tell Colonel Grant you've established a 'home away from home?' No, I'm just kidding. Anything I can do for you, is there anything that you need?"

"Sir," I smiled, "you might put a fire to the feet of the 703rd Ordnance Company to get those 7th Regiment tanks back here."

We shook hands, saluted, and he was gone. As I returned to the revetment, walking up the slight incline from the road, I noticed a heavy cloud formation to the northwest.

Eleventh Day, 1145 Hours

Late in the morning of the next day, 24 July 1952, I received a call from the executive officer, Major Caudell. He instructed me to attend a battalion officer's call at 1400 hours to be held in the Headquarters Company mess tent. This was my first officer's call with the 2nd Battalion. They are not held very frequently because it was risky pulling officers off the line and away from their units. I reasoned that it had to be something pretty important—but what? Enemy action was limited to patrols, as were our activities; was there a new offensive by the Chinese or us? Maybe the truce talks at Panmunjom had come to a conclusion. Or, who knows—my thoughts trailed off.

The mess tent looked full, but I knew that not all the 2nd Battalion officers were present. Some, by necessity, had to be left behind with the various units. I had my map board and pocket notebook with me in the event the presentation got really detailed. Promptly at 1400 hours Major Caudell stepped up close to the podium and waited. There was a stir at the entrance to the tent, and then the 2nd Battalion CO entered. Major Caudell shouted "Attention!" and the assembled officers rose as a body.

Major Crain stepped up to the podium, paused to look over his officers, and said, "Please be seated, gentlemen. I'm glad to see you all looking so well. My portion of this presentation will be short. Let me get to the heart of the matter." He paused for emphasis and then said, "The 7th Infantry Regiment is being taken off the line and placed in I (First) Corps reserve!" There was an audible sound from the assembled officers. "While there we will undergo intensive training, receive needed replacements, and upgrade our equipment." He let his message sink in and then continued, "We will be replaced by the 15th Infantry Regiment. The relief will take place over the twenty-seventh and twenty-eighth of this month. Advance party personnel from the 15th Infantry will be here on the twenty-sixth.[6] Our battalion has two days to get ready. There is a lot of coordinating to be done to make this a smooth transition with the 15th Infantry. I want to make this move a seamless transfer. I'm counting on you for your best effort. The battalion staff is here to answer all of your questions. Thank you for your attention—and good luck!"

We came to attention as Major Crain departed. Major Caudell took over the podium and said, "Resume your seats, please." He commenced with the details of the transfer and brought in the various staff officers, as needed, to fill in answers to questions for which he did not have a ready response.

My immediate thought, in view of this pleasant information, was that I was to be relieved by the 15th Tank Company. Even if available, there was little point to sending 7th Tank Company tanks forward. I paid close attention to the plan for the coming move. The role of the

2nd Platoon was to depart Hill 199 on the twenty-ninth at 1500 hours. The reason for being one day behind the main elements in effecting the transfer was traffic control. The vehicle congestion on the twenty-seventh and the twenty-eighth was expected to be very heavy, with units moving in and out on a single road—the only road. Mixing incoming and outgoing tanks into that traffic flow could introduce a traffic jam of major proportions. The twenty-ninth sounded O.K. to me. I almost laughed out loud reflecting on the irony of being ultimately relieved by the 15th Infantry Regiment tanks. The focus had been on the repair of the 7th Tank Company tanks as a preliminary activity leading to the relief of my platoon. Now that repair was irrelevant to leaving Hill 199.

When the officer's call ended, I made my way to the tank perimeter to break the news to Holt and the tank crews. Holt and the crews already knew about the 7th leaving and the 15th replacing them. The news had spread like a wildfire throughout the 2nd Battalion. I told him we would discuss the details of the transfer tomorrow; meanwhile, 1500 hours on the twenty-ninth was our "D" day—departure day.

4
Stuck in the Mud

I reflected on yesterday's news. Here we were in our twelfth day up front, and we still had four more to go before we could move out. The 2nd Battalion CO had given the units two days to prepare to move, which they would probably need. I thought that if pressed hard, I could move the 2nd Platoon out in twenty minutes. This must be some form of Murphy's Law: *The quickest shall always be last.*

My concern was how best to use the next four days. The platoon had settled into a daily routine of housekeeping activities; crew cross training, such as gunnery and vehicle maintenance; regular hours; hot or warm chow depending on whether one was at the top or bottom of Hill 199; an occasional mortar attack; and coping with the hot and dusty environment. Life was not too different from being in bivouac back at Charlie Company. The main difference, and it was a big one, was being face-to-face with the enemy. We could not see him, but he was there—just beyond the MLR at the next ridge. Routine though they were, our days were always overshadowed by the threat of Chinese intentions. Those intentions, you realized after sifting through all the rationalizations, were murderous. I decided to keep to the routine; nothing novel suggested itself as I examined the limited options at my disposal.

Later in the day, during our routine radio communication check, Holt volunteered an interesting piece of information: the Imjin River had risen and was now too high to be fordable with a quarter-ton. I thought about that for a moment and concluded that it must be due to rain up north. That was Holt's view also. At the moment, in the sunshine, the significance escaped me. A light rain started that night.

The elements, rain or shine, hot or cold, present unique problems to the soldier. Each condition must be faced and overcome in tandem with performing the assigned mission and duties. The weather is just one more part of the puzzle of doing the job effectively. Rain brought its own caseload of difficulties. The daily tasks of life became burdensome; personal comfort dropped to a new low. Simple things, such as eating or using the latrine, became an exercise in frustration. Up on the hill, food was wet and cold, and toilet paper became a soggy mess. Life was less agreeable when performing motor stables with water running down the back of your neck. Gunnery exercises were put aside because sheets of rain masked pinpoint targets. The hex tents in the tank perimeter needed deeper ditching to improve drainage.

THIRTEENTH DAY, 0730 HOURS

By the next morning it was raining hard. It was the twenty-sixth of July, and advance elements of the 15th Infantry Regiment began to arrive. The main party would be here on the twenty-seventh and twenty-eighth.[1] The disposition of the battalions of the 15th Infantry Regiment was to be the same as that of the 7th Infantry. The 2nd and 3rd battalions would be on the line, and the 1st Battalion would be in regimental reserve. The Greek Expeditionary Battalion would remain in place. I received a telephone call from Captain Hornstein late in the morning. He had two items he wanted to pass on to me. First, the heavy rain we were experiencing would last about one week. It was the monsoon season in Korea, and with that rain came evidence of heightened enemy activity—the Chinese were likely to try to use the rain and its accompanying difficulties to their advantage. In both cases I was now on notice to recognize the potential problems and make adjustments accordingly. Second, he said the direct-fire support delivered by the 2nd Platoon over the last thirteen days had made a very real contribution to the 2nd Battalion by taking the fight to the enemy. He then wished me good luck and a safe return to Charlie Company.

I immediately called Holt and filled him in on my conversation with the S-3. I directed him to check the ditching around the tents and to be especially watchful at night. My concerns now were keeping the tanks well maintained and the men comfortable. I asked Holt whether he had ever heard of a monsoon season in Korea. He said it was news to him. It was news to me also.

The road up the hill was getting sloppy. I wondered what it would be like after a week of rain and normal vehicular traffic. The rain was coming down in sheets. Monsoon season! No one had ever mentioned it. It then occurred to me that the reason I had not known of this seasonal condition was the personnel rotation system. Those who had experienced this season last year were long gone from Korea. There was no one in the unit, Charlie Company for instance, to pass on the oral history to newcomers. The rule was nine months up front, and then you were rotated out of Korea to the United States—just enough time to wipe clean the collective memory of the unit. I brought the two crews on the hill to my bunker to brief them as I had Holt. Again, maintenance of the tanks was the highest priority, followed by personal protection from the weather. I instructed both crews to inspect and improve the drainage around the bunkers.

Another mortar barrage arrived at about 2300 hours. The explosions shook the ground and rattled the support columns. I held my hands tightly to my ears, and the phrase "heightened enemy activity" came to mind. Very timely and appropriate, I thought. And "welcome!" to the Heavy Weapons Company of the 15th Infantry Regiment. Their advance party had arrived late in the afternoon. The shaky support columns of the bunker were a troublesome thought. If the ground got soaked enough, the stability of the bunker might become a safety issue. I made my guard inspection round, and as I returned from the "22" tank I wondered again whether the tanks were the target of the mortars. My final thought before turning in was that I had had just about enough frontline exposure for the month of July. I was ready and primed to be relieved on the twenty-ninth.

~

Captain Charles D. Neilson, commanding officer of G Company, 2nd Battalion, 15th Infantry Regiment, arrived at the MLR at mid-afternoon on 26 July 1952. He was there with his advance party to firm up the details of relieving G Company, 7th Infantry, the following day. Command and control issues were his main areas of interest. He would discover that G Company's sector of responsibility on the MLR extended far beyond the scope prescribed for a deployed company of infantry. The textbook rules for the maneuver of infantry formations were being substantially stretched. One member of the advance party was Master Sergeant John T. Burke, 2nd Platoon, who was assigned to occupy Outpost Kelly on 27 July 1952. Burke would be in command of the platoon in the absence of First Lieutenant Richard L. Hoff, who was due to return from R&R in several days.[2]

With a guide from the 7th Infantry, Master Sergeant Burke made a reconnaissance of the outpost. It was late in the afternoon as the two infantrymen moved through the safe lane outside the MLR and made their way to Outpost Kelly. Normally, the trip would be made during the hours of darkness to avoid being observed by the Chinese and attracting enemy mortar and artillery fire. Now, though, it was raining hard, and the likelihood of two men being seen was remote. The trail across the one thousand yards of open ground was becoming soft, making walking difficult. The south slope of Kelly was becoming slick.

Burke had been on outpost duty before, but this was his first trip to Outpost Kelly. The layout on the hilltop was much like other U.S. Army fortifications. A trench encircled the high point of the hill, which was a slightly rounded dome. Outside the trench was a screen of barbwire intermixed with concertina wire. The entrenchment was in the form of an oval with the major axis about sixty yards long, running generally east and west. The minor axis was about forty yards in length. There were several large pits with no overhead cover inside the trench line. Burke was told there was an antipersonnel minefield outside the barbwire on the north slope of Kelly, but it was unmarked, and no one knew precisely where the mines were located. Outpost Kelly was designed to accommodate a platoon of infantry.

Back at the MLR with the advance party, Burke described the situation at Kelly to Captain Neilson. The plan, as it developed, would place the 2nd Platoon on the outpost during the hours of darkness on 27 July 1952 and relieve the 7th Infantry platoon. G Company would be responsible from that time forward for manning Outpost Kelly.

Fourteenth Day, 0800 Hours

At motor stables the next morning, 27 July 1952, the end of our second week, we discovered the first casualty to the 2nd Platoon. The quarter-ton had been hit. Nestled in its protective shelter next to the road, the vehicle showed two jagged slashes in the left-side body panel near the engine and a shattered windshield on the driver's side. The damage was only superficial, however. I instructed our platoon mechanic to take his bedding and duffel and the quarter-ton down the hill and join Holt at the perimeter. As vulnerable as the vehicle was, and with the road becoming treacherous, there was little point in keeping the vehicle on the hill. With the intensity of the rain, I reckoned that within two days a wheeled vehicle would not be able to negotiate the hill either up or down.

The mortar attack the previous night set me thinking that perhaps the tanks, in their revetments, were too provocative by presenting a target in full view. Actually, I still did not know whether the Chinese were shooting at the tanks or the Heavy Mortar Company or just sending in some H&I fire. In any event I had both tanks moved out of their revetments and backed down the slope far enough to conceal them from Chinese observation. The men laid dunnage, loose material such as branches from shrubs and packing boards, under the tracks to ensure good traction later. The soil was becoming saturated and turning into a clinging, gluelike material.

Shortly after noon chow I received a call to report to the CO, 2nd Battalion, 7th Infantry Regiment. I was not told the subject matter. All morning, there had been a steady stream of vehicles bringing the 15th Infantry Heavy Mortar Company personnel up the hill and taking 7th Infantry personnel down the hill. I presumed I was to get detailed instructions on my relief by the 15th Tank Company. I was able to hitch a ride on a two-and-one-half-ton truck going down the hill.

The 2nd Battalion area had been roughly divided into two sections: one for the 15th personnel coming in and the other for 7th personnel going out. The wet ground was churned and rutted from continuous vehicle traffic. Several days ago it had been hard baked and dusty; now it was ankle-deep mud. I made my way through the moving and standing troop formations to the CP bunker. Inside, the glow of several Coleman gasoline lanterns cast sharp shadows against the walls. I saw a small group of people in the room, all wearing ponchos and looking soaked to the skin. The only person I recognized was Captain Hornstein; we nodded recognition to each other. No one was speaking. Major Crain was on the phone. In short order he finished the conversation, looked up, saw me, and motioned me forward. I stepped to the table and said, "Sir, Lieutenant Siewert reports as ordered."

"Siewert, we're really rushed today, so I'll make this brief. This damn rain has made the transfer of responsibility doubly difficult," he said, almost as an aside. "Rain is the reason you're here, and it's the reason you'll be staying here. The roads are becoming a mess everywhere, and I Corps has prohibited track-laying vehicles from using the roads.[3] The 15th Tank Company is still back at Camp Casey. Your platoon is to remain in place, and when I leave here tomorrow you'll be passed to the operational control of the 2nd Battalion of the 15th Infantry." He smiled and said, "We'll make an infantryman out of you yet. Any questions?"

As soon as he had said, "Rain is the reason you're here," I knew that the 2nd Platoon was stuck—stuck in the mud.

"No questions, sir. It's hard to argue with I Corps logic."

"I've been pleased to have you in my command." He held out his hand, and we shook hands. "Good luck to you and your platoon!"

"Thank you, sir!" I took a step back, came to attention, saluted, and departed the bunker. I went immediately to the tank perimeter to see Holt and the tank crews to bring them up to date on the ebb and flow of the 2nd Platoon.

As I walked up the hill I considered the circumstances leading to the present situation. This had to be the ultimate change in plans and the lowest point in expectations. A mission that had started with an expected duration of "several days" was now into its second week, and there was no end in sight. Plans had been modified and adjusted over and over. I was conscious of being involved in a lesson learned, but it had not quite formed a clear message yet. I put those hazy thoughts aside and concentrated on the immediate problem of two immobile tanks stuck in the mud on a Korean ridgeline. My focus was on the safety of the tanks and their crews. Until the rain stopped and the road could be restored, the tanks were incapable of going anywhere. In the past a hazardous situation could always be handled by putting the tank in reverse and departing the area. That option was no longer available. It was a situation I had never faced before—there was no escape route open. Mentally I drew up a short list of the hazards facing the tanks on the hill. Foremost, and dwarfing all others, was what to do if the Chinese made an all-out attack and penetrated the MLR. I recalled the depth of the Chinese assault on Little Gibraltar, Hill 355, last November. I had two courses of action open to me. First, we could fight the Chinese from the tanks; we had a lot of firepower. This option was feasible only if a screen of U.S. infantry was maintained around the tanks, however. Unsupported, immobile tanks would be vulnerable to close-in enemy action. Second, isolated and unsupported, the tanks could be abandoned. The crews, of course, would deploy on foot and move with our infantry. The three tanks at the foot of the hill would use the existing road to evacuate and continue to support the infantry with direct fire. On the hill, the abandoned tanks would have to be disabled to prevent their use by the enemy. Disabling a tank was relatively simple: disassemble the machine guns and throw away the components, ignite a thermite grenade in the cannon breech and render the gun useless by melting the steel, and remove key electrical components from the engine. Abandoning the tanks was a dismal prospect. Being stuck in the mud, I was learning, had a high risk potential.

It was obvious that the rain was causing ever-mounting problems to the smooth transfer of responsibility from the 7th to the 15th. Command and control communication links were failing. Logistic support was tied to a single road, the MSR, which crossed the Imjin River at White Front Bridge. Our survivability was tied to the passage of vehicles over that bridge. The current report was that the Imjin had risen twenty feet in twelve hours.[4] The threat posed by the loss of the bridge was unthinkable. Rising water, at flood stage, was now challenging the structural integrity of the bridge. With binoculars we could watch the floating parade of junk from our hilltop; trees, dead animals, houses, parts of bridges, boxes, and large drums flowed out of the north. The variety was endless. When the debris got to the bridge, it would collide with the trestle bents, the main supports. There it would cling and accumulate and grow in mass, and the force of the rushing water would be magnified against the supports. As you can well imagine, all traffic over the bridge was controlled. The resulting slowdown created a traffic jam that was monumental. To lose the bridge would be catastrophic; a large frontage of the 3rd Infantry Division would have to depend on less-efficient routes for troop movement and supplies. Our dependency on the bridge for effective operations was total. The engineers were doing everything in their power to preserve the structure. And part of this preservation effort was delegated to Charlie Company, 64th Tank Battalion.

As a small footnote to history, let it be recorded that a platoon of tanks was deployed along the banks of the Imjin River, near the bridge, to break up the floating debris with cannon fire before it reached the bridge. First Lieutenant Stanley Joltan, 4th Platoon, was given the mission of destroying large floating objects with 90m/m HE rounds. His platoon faced no easy task to take under fire, and hit, fast-moving trees and houses. It was a very difficult gunnery exercise. Although Stan's platoon was successful in breaking up much of the debris it shot at, he was directed to cease fire after two days of effort. His firing, it turned out, presented an unacceptable danger to the 15th Infantry regimental headquarters area. It seemed that occasionally a shell would miss the target, fail to detonate when it struck the water surface, skip off the water, and then explode when it hit solid ground in the distance. One such shell exploded in the 1st Battalion Headquarters reserve area. There were no injuries, but an HE fragment punctured the air mattress of the bunk reserved for Major John Eisenhower, son of General Dwight D. Eisenhower. Major Eisenhower was scheduled to join the 1st Battalion, 15th Infantry Regiment, on 2 August 1952.[5]

FIFTEENTH DAY, 1000 HOURS

The road up Hill 199 became impassable to wheeled vehicles the next day. Three days of monsoon rain was taking its toll. Among the casualties was the "garage," parts of which fell into the road. The result was a drenched, forlorn pile of timbers and sandbags. A party of KSCs carried off some of the timbers later in the day (figure 8). Parts of the road sim-

Figure 8. Monsoon rain. A Korean Service Corps work party is salvaging timber from our collapsed "garage," seen in the foreground. Note that the mud is up to their knees.

ply washed away as runoff water formed a streambed along the road and cascaded downhill. The ditches were overwhelmed. A short distance from the "21" bunker, at a curve, a gap in the road had widened to several feet due to the erosion caused by the rushing water. Over time it would only get worse. From this day on, all supplies would be delivered by foot on the backs of the KSC. At noon the chow was delivered in the usual marmite cans, but it had lost much of its warmth due to the long hike from the mess tent, which was now the Headquarters Company mess tent, 2nd Battalion, 15th Infantry Regiment. I knew that very little other than food and water would be coming up the hill. Our road had become 350 yards of shin-deep mud. Prior to the monsoon, as routine daily maintenance, we had always topped off the gas tanks and filled the ammunition wells of the tanks. For the present, the tanks were well provisioned and not an immediate concern.

Being stuck on a hill with two tanks brought to mind being stuck elsewhere in Korea. The vision of a rice paddy rose in my consciousness. Charlie Company, 64th Tank Battalion, had been on a company-size training exercise in the "Playground" area. It was mid-May, and the weather and ground conditions were excellent. I was anxious to reach the 2nd Platoon objective in a timely manner, so I elected to leave the trail we were on and cross over a large rice paddy. What had started out to be a shortcut soon turned into a time-consuming lesson in retrieving a tank stuck in the mud. Up to the point where we entered the rice paddy, the ground conditions for tank maneuvers had been excellent. I translated this experience to an expectation that the rice paddy would be equally trafficable. I was wrong. I was very wrong.

I had directed the lead tank, the "23" tank, to climb the bank of the paddy and cross to the other side. The remainder of the platoon would then follow. After thirty yards of forward motion the tank came to a helpless stop. It was belly down in the paddy, with its tracks spinning uselessly as they churned mud. Haste makes waste, I thought. I had issued a really ill-considered order. I instructed the tank commander to stand by and await the return of the platoon, at which time we would free him. The platoon continued its mission.

At the conclusion of the company exercise, we returned to the stranded tank. My plan was to use the other tanks in the platoon to pull the "23" tank out of the mud. This solution, a simple, straightforward plan, was clouded by a problem of maneuvering room in the limited terrain available for towing. It was obvious that one tank would be inadequate to make the pull; two would be required. With two tanks in tandem for a straight pull, however, the available real estate left a scant ten yards before the lead tank faced a steep ravine. We realized that the stuck tank would have to be pulled in short increments. After each short pull, the tanks in tandem were returned to their starting position. Wallowing in mud, crewmen manhandled the towing cables, which were shortened accordingly and reconnected. The towing process was repeated many times until, finally, the "23" tank was free. Everyone in the platoon, especially me, got the message. Do not attempt to traverse a rice paddy with a tank! I never tried to cross a rice paddy again. Mud and dust—the hallmarks of a tanker.

Around 1300 hours I was called and told to report to the 2nd Battalion CP. The call was not unexpected. The 15th Infantry was to assume responsibility for this sector on the twenty-eighth, today. I presumed that the CO of the 2nd Battalion wanted to close up all the loose ends of the transfer, and the 2nd Platoon, Charlie Company, 64th Tank Battalion, was one of the loose ends. Walking downhill was hard going—I knew it would be doubly tough later going back uphill. Inside the CP entrance I told a sergeant who I was and that the CO was expecting me. While I waited, he went to the rear of the bunker where three officers were seated.

"Come in, Lieutenant!" It was a deep-throated shout.

I advanced to the group, stood before the battalion commander, saluted, and said, "Lieutenant Siewert reports to the commanding officer." Lieutenant Colonel Herbert F. Roye returned the salute.

"Glad to meet you, Siewert." He then pointed to the other officers. "This is Major Morrison, my executive officer, and this is Major Alphson, my S-3."

I nodded to them and said, "Good afternoon, gentlemen."

"Siewert, take a chair. By the way, what is your first name?"

"It's Jack, sir."

"Well, Jack, as you can see, we're not quite settled in yet. I understood from Major Crain that you've been here a while. As with the 7th, you're now under the operational control of the 2nd Battalion, 15th Infantry Regiment. I haven't seen any formal orders to the effect of transferring you, but your tank platoon is now part of the 2nd Battalion. What are you doing on top of that hill?"

"Sir, my mission is to provide direct-fire support for infantry operations. There is a good field of fire up there." I did not know Lieutenant Colonel Roye, so I was careful with my answer. He seemed like a very open, easy-to-approach person. I continued, "Until yesterday I was on the hill awaiting my relief by the 15th Tank Company. The I Corps directive on keeping track-laying vehicles off the roads has put me and the 15th Tank Company on hold."[6]

"Jack, believe me, the roads are really bad. Tank traffic would make them impassable. What are those three tanks doing at the foot of the hill?"

"Colonel, when the platoon came forward two weeks ago, I planned to put all the tanks on Hill 199. That idea did not work out." There was a lot left unsaid in my response. I was still not sure of how open I could be, and I did not want to sound flippant.

"O.K. Tomorrow I want you to get together with Major Alphson and give him the details of your firing activities for the last two weeks. You're the only one left around here that knows what's been going on before my battalion got here. Any questions, anything my staff can do?"

"Yes, sir, there is the matter of logistic support for the platoon. I'd like to keep the same arrangement that I had with the 7th. Whenever it's convenient, I'd like to get together with your staff members."

He nodded assent and said, "You can set up a mutual schedule with the staff members. Give them a call in the morning. Anything else? No? I'm glad to have you here. I'll be up to inspect your position soon. I'm interested in those fields of fire."

The meeting was over. As I rose from the table, I addressed Major Morrison and Major Alphson, saying, "Pleased to have met you, gentlemen." I stood to attention, saluted the CO, and said, "Thank you, sir!" I stepped outside the bunker and into a torrential downpour.

Back on top of the hill I made my way to the CP of the newly arrived Heavy Mortar Company, 15th Infantry Regiment. The purpose of my visit was to meet the new CO. Inside the bunker, except for new faces, nothing had changed. When the 7th moved out, they left much behind. The switchboard, situation map, Coleman lanterns, desks and chairs, cots, and other pieces of equipment were left standing when the 7th walked out the door. I was sure, however, that the 7th Heavy Mortar Company retained the mortars and other weapons. Those items had serial numbers on them and were carried in the company property book— somebody had signed for them and was responsible for them. I spent only a moment with the CO, Captain Leonard Schwartz, because he was very busy. We agreed to meet the next day and work out the details of cohabiting Hill 199.

A Chinese mortar barrage struck Hill 199 around 2000 hours. This barrage was a long one—a lot of incoming rounds. I discovered I could partially mask my fear by counting the explosions. It kept my mind active and diverted so that mindless fear would not completely take over my being. On or about forty rounds was my estimate. I am never going to get used to this, I thought. Our bunker appeared sound in spite of three days of soaking rain. I think the fact that the roof showed no leaks gave the impression of structural soundness. For evening chow the KSCs had dropped off extra cans of water and cases of C rations; each case had canned meals for five men for one day (5-in-1). It looked like we would be preparing our own meals for a while. Each tank crew had a small gasoline-burning stove to heat the meals. We could also use the tank exhaust system as an alternative if the engine was running. A C ration can fit easily into the exhaust tail pipe, and the hot exhaust gases would quickly heat a can of food. To keep the cans from exploding when overheated, we punctured the top of them. This was an important step in meal preparation—our constant companions, the rats, now seemed more numerous, and we did not need anything else, such as uncovered food, to attract even more of them. Most likely the rain was filling up their tunnels and nests, forcing them to seek drier shelter. We made every effort to maintain a scrupulously clean bunker to avoid attracting rats. We policed up all food and waste and covered our sanitary fill and latrine with bleach and dirt daily. Even so, the rats were with us constantly and could be heard squeaking and scurrying throughout the day and night.

At 2130 hours the rumble of distant explosions penetrated the bunker. The noise was not uncommon, but the volume and duration caught my attention. Suddenly, Sergeant Davis, who was on guard duty in the tank, appeared in the bunker entrance and said, "Lieutenant, all hell is breaking loose on the OPLR. I think it's Kelly!"

5
Outpost Kelly Is Lost

Rain ran off my poncho and into my boots. In my haste to observe the action on Outpost Kelly, I had not bothered to lace the boots up. My binoculars were not much help in the rain and darkness, either. Standing in the revetment I could see, dimly, quick flashes of explosions concentrated on Kelly. The roar of reports piling on each other in rapid succession was continuous, but muffled by the rain. I had been standing in the revetment only a few moments when there came the sharp cough of our 4.2-inch mortar tubes launching a salvo. I am witnessing a long enemy barrage, I thought. What was going on? Probably preparation for an assault on the outpost by the Chinese, I reasoned. All the racket and commotion out there, sixteen hundred yards away, was the combined result of both Chinese and U.S. shelling. Did it mean more than an assault on the outpost? Could this be the prelude to a general assault on our lines? The timing could not be better for the Chinese. The 15th Infantry Regiment had relieved the 7th Infantry and just this day had assumed responsibility for the left flank of the 3rd Infantry Division. Turmoil and confusion accompany such an event. Troops new to the terrain and unfamiliar with the location of their specific areas of responsibility were vulnerable to indecision. Surprise, catching your enemy flat-footed, was an important element in a successful assault. How much did the Chinese know about the change of commands and the transfer of responsibility?

I sent Sergeant Davis back to alert both the "21" and the "22" tank crews to stand by in their bunkers. Action might be imminent. The muffled roar continued. I watched for another minute and then returned to the bunker to call the S-3. The 2nd Battalion switchboard did not respond immediately; when it did, and I asked for the S-3, I was told all lines to Operations were busy. I went to the other telephone and called Sergeant First Class Holt and filled him in on what I knew. I also instructed him to have his crews standing by. My next stop was the Heavy Mortar Company CP. If I could not get through to the S-3, I knew my next step was to contact Captain Schwartz because he would have some hard information. Those 4.2-inch mortar fire missions were being directed somewhere. I left the bunker and slogged over to the CP.

It was busy! The fire missions that were being sent down to the mortar platoon in the form of preplanned defensive concentrations were based on contingency plans. These fire missions were conducted at the request of personnel on Outpost Kelly and were triggered by events as they unfolded. On a field phone Captain Schwartz was talking to the S-3. I watched and listened and caught the phrase "fire the box."[1] This meant a salvo would place mortar rounds on all sides of Kelly below the barbwire. In addition to our mortars, a battery of the 39th Field Artillery was firing a concentration against the Chinese on the north slope of Kelly.

I moved back against the wall, out of the way, and watched the operation in progress. It was well ordered and purposeful, I thought, but somehow old-fashioned or dated. Bunkers, trenches, barbwire, telephone wire, switchboards, and telephones just did not fit the image of the modern army of the 1950s. Where were the radio links? The scene I was looking at would fit very comfortably into the Battle of the Marne, France, in July 1918. It was this battle in which the 3rd Infantry Division earned the proud title, "Rock of the Marne," the division motto. With a little imagination you could picture the German Imperial Army poised just beyond the MLR, ready to launch their 1918 spring offensive.

Where, indeed, were the radios? The simple fact was that the radios issued to the infantry units could not be relied on. This applied particularly in wet weather. The radios issued to artillery and armor units worked just fine. But the recently issued PRC-10 field radio set, dedicated for use by the infantry, was a nonstarter, a flop, in the monsoon rains. The only viable fallback option left to the infantry was field wire and telephones.

There was a steady crosscurrent of conversations in the CP. All the telephones were manned. No information was coming from Outpost Kelly because the line was out. What we knew about Kelly came from G Company on the MLR, and the information was sketchy. At this point the contest for Kelly had been in heated progress for about thirty minutes. Finally, Captain Schwartz, phone pressed to his head, broadcasted with a shout to the whole bunker, "Kelly is lost—stragglers are coming into G Company now!"

The details of the loss became clear later as the events on Kelly were reconstructed. The chronological sequence of events that led to the capture of Outpost Kelly by the Chinese was revealed by interrogation of the participants. It was a simple story.

～

Eighteen men under the command of Master Sergeant John T. Burke, 2nd Platoon, G Company, manned the outpost; three were in a listening post (LP), downhill next to the trail. A listening post has the purpose of providing early warning of an approaching force. The listening post, which comprises a small number of men, frequently engages the approaching force with small-arms fire to halt or stall an advance. Burke had been posted to the hill on the twenty-seventh of July as an element of the relief of the 7th Infantry by the 15th. A force of twenty-one men, led by First Lieutenant Sherwin Arculis, 1st Platoon, G Company, was scheduled to relieve the outpost at 2130 hours on the twenty-eighth of July. By 2030 hours Lieutenant Arculis had passed through the MLR and moved through the safe lane in our defensive minefield. His detail made its way in steady rain toward Kelly. The route was muddy and slippery. About halfway up the slope to the crest of Kelly, on the left side of the trail, a sergeant and five men with a machine gun relieved those at the LP. The relief column proceeded up the trail. Then, with the head of the relief column on Kelly, the remainder strung out over thirty yards of trail, the Chinese hit Outpost Kelly.[2] Ambush!

The Chinese assault was well planned and executed. An estimated two reinforced platoons, in concealment, flanked the trail to the east and west. To the north another platoon lay in wait to attack the top of

Kelly. The assault on Lieutenant Arculis and the relief detail at 2130 hours was the signal for the third platoon to assault the crest from the north. Simultaneously, the Chinese launched a mortar barrage on Outpost Kelly. The Chinese, attacking Master Sergeant Burke and his men on top of the hill, moved forward through their own mortar fire. Chinese doctrine accepted friendly fire losses to achieve an objective. A concussion grenade detonated on Burke's carbine; the carbine stock broke, and he was stunned and blinded momentarily.[3] Burke was then severely wounded in the right shoulder area by a fragmentation grenade. First Lieutenant Arculis was severely wounded at about the same time. In the darkness and rain, the firefight became a confusing melee.

As he later recalled in a letter dated 31 March 2004, Colonel Sherwin Arculis stated, in part:

> Towards the end of July, the 15th Rgt relieved the 7th Rgt on the MLR.
>
> When G Co moved into the line it assumed responsibility for Outpost Kelly, so elements of one of its platoons occupied the Outpost probably 26 or 27 July. At the time, the MLR positions and the COPL [combat outpost line] were the responsibility of the 7th Rgt.
>
> This platoon led by MSG John Burke was on OP Kelly, and on 28 July my platoon was directed to conduct a night relief of Burke's platoon. I recall we left the MLR after dark and proceeded through the safe lane toward Kelly. I do not remember if someone guided us to the position of Burke's platoon or if we simply followed a known path. I do recall it was raining again making visibility quite bad and the ground muddy and slippery. There were no signs of any activity as we approached the position.
>
> I believe I met MSG Burke as we approached the hill and we relieved his rear LP.
>
> My command group had followed the point element onto the hill and I had moved up the position and was on the right side of the hill in a trench. Elements of my platoon, possibly a LMG [light machine gun], proceeded forward to the front of the position where MSG Burke was now located.

The rest of the platoon was strung out in single file coming up the hill from the valley.

The Chinese attacked at approximately 2300 with mortar, artillery and small arms during the middle of the relief and literally cut my platoon in half.

The Chinese attacked from the front against the position and at the same time made a left flank attack cutting across my platoon coming up from the valley; (An operational log reported that the position was attacked by an element moving in the saddle between OP Tessie, and another element from the rear of Kelly, and another from OP Cavite.)

I recall calling for supporting fires, "fire the box," and when the arty [artillery] flares ignited I saw a Chinese soldier standing up on the hill to our left and spraying the area with a burp gun.

(Today John Burke told me the hill was swarming with CCF [Chinese Communist forces] soldiers firing weapons and throwing grenades.)

Suddenly I was hit in the left shoulder by either indirect fire fragments or small arms fire. My radio operator was also hit and his radio became inoperative. My group was out of contact with Burke's soldiers and we could not use the radio.

There was heavy firing ahead of us, from the top of the hill, as well as to our rear. I believe MSG Burke was also wounded at this time.

My group got off the hill by going down the right slope through the several bands of barbed wire and circled back behind Kelly where we observed the fire fight and fire support. We eventually made it back to our lines.

I entered one of the bunkers where an aid man dressed my shoulder wound as well as a barbed wire cut on my left shin. I subsequently was evacuated to the Bn [battalion] aid station. At the aid station the company commander debriefed me. A doctor looked at my wounds and I was evacuated to the 8055 MASH [mobile army surgical hospital]. I was operated on at the MASH and then moved to the 25th Evacuation Hospital in Tague south of Seoul.

Master Sergeant Burke and the nine men he led fought their way off of Kelly and moved to the MLR.[4] In view of the confusion of the night fight, Burke elected to wait outside the MLR until daylight to avoid a friendly fire confrontation with our troops. Although wounded, his concern was the safekeeping of his men. They spent a long, cold, wet night waiting for first light.

~

G Company paid a high price for the combat action on the night of 28 July 1952. The casualty totals were as follows: severely wounded in action—two; lightly wounded in action—fourteen.

The Chinese held Outpost Kelly.

SIXTEENTH DAY, 0200 HOURS

Our artillery and mortars were pummeling Kelly as I returned to my bunker. The rain beat a tattoo on my helmet; I tried to collect my thoughts as I walked. In an objective sense, I thought, Kelly is part of a chess game being played with real people. The Chinese capture the outpost, so we recapture it. Or was this Chinese move merely the opening phase of a much larger assault? Subjectively, the only pertinent question was what role the 2nd Platoon would have.

Both the "21" and "22" tank crews assembled in my bunker for a briefing. A sense of personal loss was inescapable in terms of casualties and the loss of the outpost. Those were our people, and that was our hill. We were part of the 2nd Battalion, and Kelly was a piece of us. My briefing was short; I said I was sure that we would be involved in the response, whatever it was to be. Meanwhile, we would stand by and await orders. I called Holt, explained the situation as I knew it, and told him to stand by with the three other tank crews until further orders.

At 0230 hours, on the twenty-ninth of July, the telephone rang, and Operations told me to stand by for a conference call. While waiting, I rehashed in my mind the events from late the previous night. The single salient fact that stood above all others was that the loss of the outpost carried a price. The personnel casualties were just a down payment on what was to come. I could only guess what the final cost would be.

Major Alphson, the S-3, came on the line. As he went through his roster of combat and combat-support elements, we each responded with "here" when our name was called. He noted that the operation order would be verbal, that time did not permit issuing a written document. His order was concise. A platoon from F Company plus nine men from the Patrol and Ambush Platoon and five men from G Company, as guides, would retake Outpost Kelly. They would cross the MLR at 0345 hours, with the assault to commence at 0530 hours.[5] Preparatory artillery and mortar fire for twenty minutes would precede the assaulting unit, with firing to commence at 0510 hours. The tanks would place direct supporting fire on the crest of Kelly as the opportunity developed. The artillery forward observer (FO) accompanying the assault platoon would call and adjust fire as needed. Command and communication with the assault platoon and within the 2nd Battalion would be by use of field telephone using an open-line conference call network ("net"). Supplies and medical support would follow the assault element, on call. Rain was forecast to continue, and poor footing was to be expected. The 2nd Battalion CP would remain in its present location. There were a few questions, quickly answered. Mine was to confirm that the lead assault element would be displaying ground identification panels, my concern being a friendly fire incident. Ground identification panels were two-by-five-foot-long fluorescent orange cloth normally used to signal aircraft to avoid casualties by friendly fire. Prior to closing down the conference call net, the S-3 cautioned everyone to observe strict telephone etiquette for the coming assault. It was imperative that comment, cross talk, and conversation be held to an absolute minimum.

I assembled both tank crews in my bunker and briefed them. Condensed, the instructions I gave to the crews were as follows: We would wind up the engines at 0500 hours and open the SCR-508 radio net; move into the revetments at 0529 hours; await my command to fire; be alert for florescent orange panels; and be aware that contact with the 2nd Battalion would be by way of the telephone located in the "21" tank. I rang up Holt on the direct-line phone and briefed him on the platoon mission. His role was to stand by with the three crews in the perimeter, monitor the action on the SCR-508 radio net, and be prepared to replace me if I became a casualty. I told Holt, as I had told the men with me, to be sure the crews all had breakfast. I wanted everyone with a full stomach before the fight started. You fight better on a full stomach, and there was no telling when we would have time for the next meal.

Morale of the crews was high—they were more than ready for the coming action. The four days of torrential rain had made the men slightly depressed, but the prospect of action picked up their spirits. It was payback time for the mortar barrages they had endured. The daily gunnery exercises had sharpened their skills, and they knew their jobs. Now they were to get a chance to deliver the goods. We were not dealing with "suspected" targets this time; there were real, live Chinese troops on that hill. I was ready, too. Or was I? Had I forgotten something, was there an item left undone or unsaid? No, I reflected, I think I am as set as I can be. Events would soon prove me wrong.

While waiting, I tried to visualize what was coming. What would this day bring? The infantry has a tough job ahead, I thought. From the MLR they had to go downhill and then across a small valley to the foot of Kelly, about one thousand yards. Then they had to go up the south slope of Kelly to the crest, about 350 yards. All this was to be done in the rain and mud. The Chinese would likely resist our effort to regain the outpost, which meant a fight. It was here, at the line where the two forces met, where a large question had to be faced: Who would prevail?

I could not recall ever meeting First Lieutenant Lewis Kluttz from F Company, who would be leading the assault, but I knew the FO who would be with him. First Lieutenant Larry Axelrod, Field Artillery, had been with the 15th Infantry Regiment in February for Operation Snare. Two tank platoons, mine included, from Charlie Company had been up front supporting the 15th Infantry Regiment. During the week we were together, I got to know Larry Axelrod. Over time, names began to mean something; you could place a face with a name. The people you were with, however briefly, became known to you. And because you knew these people, you were drawn into those events in which they were involved. Combat action became very personal, very subjective. The involvement of my platoon to provide direct-fire support was more than just a tactical responsibility. I was assisting and helping friends, brothers, engaged in a deadly endeavor.

Of course, there was always the possibility that the Chinese had evacuated the outpost. Had they left the hill? You had to strain hard to believe that they were actually gone and that the recovery of the outpost would be bloodless. Well, we will soon find out, I thought.

SIXTEENTH DAY, 0500 HOURS

At 0500 hours the tank engines roared into life and then settled down into a husky idle. A light rain came out of the west, driven by a brisk wind. The dawn sky was still a dark gray with low scudding clouds. Ankle deep in mud, I walked around the tank to assure myself that we would not have a problem moving up the slight grade into the revetment. I settled into the turret and opened the radio net with the "22" tank and Sergeant First Class Holt. On Outpost Kelly I could hear the rain-muffled roar of the artillery and mortar preparation. The field phone, which had been moved from the bunker to the turret, rang, and the conference call network was opened. The S-3 went through his check-list; finally he came to me.

"Are the tanks in the net?" he asked.

"Here, sir!"

"O.K." he said, and moved on with his list.

Shortly the S-3 added, "Remember, keep the talk down, don't monopolize the net, only essential information. We're on a party line, and I want the assault platoon to have ready access to all the support forces."

On schedule, both tanks moved into their revetments. Outpost Kelly, sixteen hundred yards away, was smothered by a cloud of explosions from our mortar and artillery fire. Shells slammed into the top and sides of the hill. Air bursts from proximity-fused artillery rounds sprayed shrapnel into the hill below. The proximity fuse, a relatively new concept, used the principle of radar to detect the distance of the shell to the target. The preset fuse would detonate the shell at a specified distance from the target. This panorama of violence was easily seen through the curtain of rain; what could not be seen was the movement of our assaulting platoon. The infantry, in place and waiting, moved out at 0530 hours. Their movement could not be detected from Hill 199. At roughly a mile away, their uniforms blended into the mud-soaked south slope of Kelly. And there was no sign of a florescent orange panel. It did not take much imagination to visualize the difficulty of their advance. They would be heavily burdened with weapons, ammunition, and grenades as they went slipping and sliding in shin-deep mud while moving uphill and trying to maintain an offensive formation. Just keeping their rifles from becoming fouled and inoperable from mud would be a challenge. At the end of the trail, the crest of the hill, was an unenviable prospect—a firefight with an enemy that was well dug-in. If they were still there, you could be sure the Chinese had dug deep and improved the entrenchments since taking the hill. Still, they may have departed. In that case they would have scavenged what they could, deployed a few booby traps, scattered safe-conduct passes to encourage our troops to desert, and stolen away before daybreak. You could bet a month's pay that that was what each infantryman was thinking and hoping as he labored forward. Before our troops got too far uphill, I wanted to fire ranging shots at the top of Kelly to ensure we were on target. I still could see no orange panels.

My fire mission order over the radio to both tanks called for them to shoot one round of WP for ranging and then to hold fire until further orders. The preparatory fires were still under way, and an HE burst would be lost in the melee of explosions. The WP would be a brilliant white blossom, an unmistakable marker of a tank round on target.

"Fire!" I commanded. The rush of adrenaline pumping through my body was equal parts of anxiety and excitement. A racing pulse and heavy breathing—I should be in a foot race, I thought. I heard the metallic "clang" of the breechblock closing and a cry of "Up!" as the WP round was rammed into the cannon breech.

"On the way!" shouted Sergeant Gardner. The burst of the round was clearly visible to him through the telescope, so he knew he was on target. The "22" tank was also on the mark. The rain presented no difficulty with regard to our seeing Kelly. Gardner's problem was seeing specific targets on the hill, such as trenches or rifle pits. The concentration of artillery and mortar fire made anything in that cloud of destruction impossible to see. For the present, any firing the tanks did would be strictly at the top of a hill mass. I decided that, until told otherwise, our contribution would be two rounds of HE per minute from each tank. The two tanks settled into a workmanlike pace of delivering eighty pounds of explosives a minute. I reflected on what this platoon could do with three more tanks on this hill.

Signal traffic on the party-line telephone network was intermittent. The assault platoon was giving sporadic progress reports of the deployment and advance of the platoon. They had crossed the initial point (IP) at 0530 hours and had fanned out in groups of squads before starting up the hill. The supporting fires continued to shell the top of Kelly. These would soon be adjusted to the north slope to avoid "short" rounds from falling on our advancing troops. Friendly fire was a very real concern, and infantry commanders went to great lengths to ensure a cushion of safety between the troops and the striking shells. This shift to the north would also make it difficult for the Chinese to reinforce their troops on Kelly. The mortars would be adjusted on command of the assault platoon leader; the FO accompanying the platoon would adjust the artillery fire. Each FO had a radio and radioman and could talk directly to the artillery battery Fire Direction Control Center. The FO would observe and direct the strike of the shells from his position with the assaulting platoon—a high-risk type of job.

Noise from the tank engine made it difficult to hear a conversation on the phone, so I had Sergeant Davis shut off the main engine and start "Little Joe," our five-horsepower auxiliary engine and generator. About that time Gardner said, "Sir, I can't see Kelly."

"Say again, Gardner. What's wrong?"

"I can't see through the scope. There is a cloud of steam coming off the gun tube," he replied.

Good grief! Now what? I rose waist high out of the turret and stared at the gun barrel. A light, hazy cloud of vapor surrounded the barrel and drifted slowly to the right. Of course! Cold rain was hitting the barrel, which had become hotter with each successive round fired. The barrel had now reached a temperature to convert rain to vapor. Through the telescope, Kelly was now totally obscured. This situation was brand new to me. No schooling, no manuals, no training had prepared me for this situation. Eight months of continuous combat experience had never turned up this scenario. It dawned on me, suddenly, that I had never conducted sustained fire in the rain. It is another lesson learned, I thought, but the timing could not be worse. What to do?

"Gardner, we'll go to the range card!" We could quickly set up the azimuth and gunners quadrant elevation for Kelly and then continue firing using indirect-fire techniques. The azimuth, one element of indirect fire, was already set, with the 90m/m gun pointed at Kelly, but the rest of the process required more time. Prior to firing, the quadrant had to be removed from the breechblock to prevent damage from recoil; after firing, the quadrant was again placed on the breechblock to adjust the next shot mechanically. "The first round will be WP. I'll observe the strike to make sure we're on top of the hill. If we're on, you can then use the quadrant for all following shots. We'll start using your last visual setting for the gun."

I got on the tank radio and called the "22" tank; they reported the same problem. My instruction to them was the same as that given to Gardner. I dismounted from the tank, turned the field phone over to Davis to monitor, and moved twenty yards to the right to observe the WP round. Both tanks hit the top of Kelly with the first shot. Two brilliant white clouds were easily distinguished from the jumble of other explosions. The problem was solved, but at the price of the slower rate of fire. Also, the loaders of both tanks were now reaching into the magazine wells under the floor of the respective fighting compartment for HE rounds, a relatively slow process. My ten-power binoculars gave me a good view of Kelly, but I could detect no movement of the assaulting platoon.

Back at the tank Davis returned the party-line phone and said, "They've started up the hill." Suddenly, as I listened, I heard a series of sharp explosions from the phone—the handset key was being held open on Kelly. Then, "We're taking mortar fire!" It was Lieutenant Kluttz, the assault platoon leader, describing his situation.

Damn! Was Kelly still held by the Chinese? Perhaps they had evacuated, and the mortar fire was being directed from some other observation post. Hill 317 was likely; it was only twelve hundred yards away to the west. The infantry troops were being hit early, with three hundred yards still to go. Could our counterbattery radar be attempting to calculate a fix on the Chinese mortar positions for a counterbattery barrage? How well did the radar work in the rain? Meanwhile, the infantrymen were struggling up the muddy south slope of Kelly with mortar shells crashing around them. I looked in vain for the orange signal panels; they were not in sight yet. I heard more explosions from the phone. How far had they advanced? The platoon leader requested that we shift our mortar fire. The FO would do the same for the artillery fire. The assault platoon must be getting close to the top.

Our tank fire was about two rounds per minute per gun, and the loader was now pulling rounds out of the ammunition wells—the ready rack had been cleaned out. At this stage the only shells hitting Kelly were the tank 90m/m cannon rounds. I had a fleeting thought: What is the fastest sustained rate of fire this cannon can handle?

"Cease tank fire! Cease tank fire!" was the command over the phone. Whose voice was that? I was not sure, but I called "cease fire" over the radio net. Were they close to the top? The water vapor cloud off the gun tube mingled with the pouring rain. My binocular scan of the south slope strained for a show of activity. The diminished visibility revealed nothing; there was no orange signal panel. The relative quiet on Hill 199 amplified the dull roar coming from Kelly. Obviously, enemy mortars were still coming in. I listened to the field phone with a sense of suddenly becoming an onlooker; there was nothing more for the tanks to contribute. My watch read 0600 hours. A half-hour had gone by since we opened fire. All I could do was listen as a bystander.

～

Considering the conditions, First Lieutenant Kluttz's infantry platoon had made good progress. They had crossed the IP at 0530 hours, on schedule, with no form of resistance from the Chinese. The assault platoon, in a shallow diamond formation of rifle squads, straddled the trail leading to the crest of Kelly. They needed to cover 350 yards to get to the top of the hill. As they mounted the hill, our mortar and artillery preparation was audible and getting louder to them with each yard they advanced. Now that they were on the upslope, the difficulty of getting good footing became magnified. Walking had been awkward in the flat valley between the MLR and the base of Kelly, but here on the slope, it was doubly difficult. For many, the normal stance was on all fours; the advance was literally being made at a crawl.

It was at this stage of the advance that the lead element of the platoon was presented with a stunning surprise. A loud cry was heard twenty yards in front of the squad. The squad halted, alert and at the ready, to meet this unexpected event. A U.S. soldier, Private First Class James MacArthur, cautiously rose from the ground in front of the squad leader. MacArthur, a member of Master Sergeant Burke's platoon, had been part of the LP located downslope on the left side of the trail. When the enemy ambush occurred, the LP had been overrun by the assaulting Chinese. From 2130 hours on 28 July 1952 to 0530 hours on 29 July 1952, MacArthur had feigned death at the LP.[6] It had been a harrowing experience. After making sure that MacArthur was physically capable, Lieutenant Kluttz directed him to return to the MLR.

About a quarter of the way up, the platoon encountered the initial resistance of the Chinese: a mortar attack. The concentration formed a curtain slightly to the rear of the assault platoon. It was a near miss. Shortly, another mortar barrage came in and landed close to the right of the platoon. The Chinese were making defensive adjustments. At 150 yards from the top of Kelly, Lieutenant Kluttz and the FO called for a shift of our artillery and mortar fire to the north. The platoon gathered itself to make a final rush to take Kelly. They advanced a few yards, and then the lead elements began to take small-arms and automatic-weapons fire from the crest. This event settled the question of whether the Chinese intended to occupy and hold Outpost Kelly. The Chinese were in the trenches. Return fire by the platoon was weak; disabled rifles, having been dragged uphill and choked with mud, malfunctioned. It was 0600 hours, and the advance was stalled.

The platoon was in an exposed position and vulnerable to the mounting small-arms fire from the top of Kelly. Reluctantly, the platoon fell back. About two hundred yards downslope, the contour of the terrain offered limited protection from the small-arms fire, and here the platoon took cover. It was 0620 hours.[7]

Lieutenant Kluttz made a critical assessment of his situation and requested that friendly mortar and tank fire resume hitting the top of Kelly; the FO did the same with the artillery fire. Before the day would end, more than one thousand shells would be placed on Kelly. To continue his attack, Lieutenant Kluttz needed help. The platoon did not have the means to clean the fouled rifles. On the party line he called for clean weapons to replace those in the hands of his riflemen. He also needed medical corpsmen and litter bearers to carry out his wounded. He was told a KSC work party would be formed and dispatched as quickly as possible and that until this assistance arrived he was to hold his present position. As exposed as the platoon was, the enemy mortars ceased firing. It was probable that the Chinese had lost sight of the platoon in the driving rain and believed that the assault had been repulsed and our troops were in retreat. During the wait for the KSC work party, our artillery and mortar fire grew in volume. Tank fire was held for the next assault.

The KSC work party, having endured several Chinese mortar concentrations when moving from the MLR to the hill, arrived at 1030 hours. While clean rifles were distributed and arrangements made to evacuate the wounded, Lieutenant Kluttz reviewed his situation. After several hours of intense bombardment, one could reasonably expect a degrading of the Chinese ability to resist a determined assault; perhaps they had even withdrawn from the crest.

The assault platoon quickly organized for their advance to the top. The bombardment of artillery and mortar fire was shifted off the crest to the north. The tank fire was stopped. The footing had been poor several hours ago, but it was much worse now. More than that, the approach to the crest of Kelly was a grade that became increasingly steep. The closer a person got to the crest, the steeper it became. The pace of the platoon bogged down in the impossible footing, and, at fifty yards from the summit, the lead squad came under small-arms fire. The Chinese were back or perhaps had never left. As they lay in the mud, the platoon realized that the volume of small-arms fire directed at them included automatic weapons, soon followed by a mortar concentration. This was an untenable place. It was here, on the second attempt to take the hill, that Lieutenant Lewis Kluttz died leading his riflemen. The men in the platoon broke contact with the enemy, gathered up their casualties, and withdrew down the hill.[8] It was 1130 hours.

⁓

The participation of the 2nd Platoon in this combat action had been as intimate as possible, short of being on the slope leading up to Kelly. Our tank direct-fire support had been continuous and on target from the moment the assault platoon crossed the IP. Every command, every request, every status report had been monitored on the party line. The crash of every enemy mortar shell had been heard. In a real sense we had been on the slope leading up to the top of Kelly. Now I realized that I was emotionally drained. The participation of the tanks in the assault had loaded my system with adrenaline; now, the exhilaration was washed away by a failed mission, a costly failed mission. Since 2130 hours on the twenty-eighth of July to 1130 hours on the twenty-ninth—fourteen hours—we had lost Outpost Kelly and failed to recover the hill. Two men were dead, and twenty-three were wounded.[9] What was it going to take to get Kelly back?

Around noon all elements of the operation were told to stand down. The two crews on Hill 199 had a lot to do. They had to clean and maintain the tank cannons, carry out motor stables, police up the brass shell casings, and then move the tanks out of their revetments. I wanted the tanks out of sight of the Chinese. After the chores had been completed, I had the two crews assemble in the "21" bunker. I told them that the support they had provided that day had been very professional, to the highest standards of the service. What I did not tell them was the thought that was gnawing at the back of my head: in spite of all that everyone had done, it was not enough.

Rain dripped down my neck as I stood in the revetment staring at Kelly. I wondered: What comes next?

6
The Fight for Outpost Kelly

Sixteenth Day, 1400 Hours

An after-action conference was called at 1400 hours for all company commanders and combat-support elements. We assembled in the Operations bunker. It was a somber gathering.

This meeting was a critique, a review, of the assault. Lieutenant Colonel Roye opened the meeting by stating that 15th Regiment had directed that Outpost Kelly would be retaken. He was to attend a planning meeting at 1630 hours to examine the present situation and develop a new plan for the recovery of Outpost Kelly. Brigadier General Charles L. Dasher, Jr., assistant division commander, would be at the meeting. It was noted, for emphasis, that Lieutenant General J. W. O'Daniel, I Corps commander, had directed that Kelly be retaken.[1] This introductory statement was made to emphasize the level of attention that the loss of Kelly commanded. One of the prime objectives of this battalion conference was to prepare Lieutenant Colonel Roye for participation in the plan to be developed later at regiment. He wanted to be totally versed in what had gone right and what had gone wrong with the aborted assault on Kelly that morning.

What had gone wrong was quite obvious. The Chinese wanted Kelly—perhaps for the simple tactical advantage, perhaps to support their position in the ongoing talks at Panmunjom. Whatever their reason, they had executed a well-planned ambush and followed it up with a vigorous defense of their newly held ground. The determined defense by the Chinese demonstrated a strong intent to hold Kelly; this was supported by the fact that more than one thousand rounds of artillery, mortar, and tank shells had been placed on Kelly during our assault and that our attack force had been repulsed twice. The strength of our attacking forces had been inadequate to overcome the will of the enemy.

What had gone right was the aggressive posture and actions of the infantrymen in the assault force. A high quality of leadership had been present. The determination of the enemy, and the weather and the poor footing in particular, had not stopped the friendly forces from trying twice to secure the hill. Two attempts, taking losses both times, showed a high level of leadership and morale.

In summary, the combat action over the last day had been a defeat by any standard of measure. There was a general consensus that a new plan must feature a larger assault force and that a better job must be done in suppressing the enemy mortar fire. The question period did not last long, and I made no contribution. We were told that we would be advised when the new plan was ready and that we could expect an Operations order to coordinate all elements involved in the plan. The CO thanked everyone for his input, and then we were dismissed. I was glad to leave, to get clear of the bunker and what the meeting had meant—a detailed review of a failure, a failed plan paid for with a lot of casualties. Outside I reflected on command responsibility and accountability. The meeting had been stressful for me, and I could only imagine how it was for the CO. The ultimate responsibility for whatever went right, or went wrong, rested with the CO. That is what command is all about. In combat, everything else being equal, it is better to be successful.

As I made my way to the tank perimeter to brief Holt, my path took me past the battalion medical aid station. It was mid afternoon, and the place was still full. Evacuation of wounded and injured had been going on since morning, but poor road conditions slowed the process. Helicopters were inoperable in this kind of weather. There were many injured men here other than those wounded by enemy action. A lot were here due to occupational hazards: an ankle broken falling down a muddy slope; a badly slashed hand while moving through barbwire; sprains and pulled ligaments incurred scrambling for cover from incoming mortar fire; and chills and fever from living soaking wet during four days of monsoon rains. A high percentage of the men at the station were KSC porters. Our casualty reports listed only the U.S. personnel; we had a tendency to forget about the Koreans, the so-called noncombatants.

Sergeant First Class Holt said he thought I looked like I had been run over by a tank. If I looked as bad on the outside as I felt on the inside, I told him, it was a good observation. My briefing was short: stand by for further orders. This had been a grim, dismal day. It was one I would like to forget, but I knew I would remember it for the rest of my life. I had been on the go, full bore, since 0200 hours, and it was now 1530 hours. The prospect of walking up Hill 199 was unappealing; I decided to postpone the hike and stay for early chow here in the 2nd Battalion area. The hot chow was a treat, and the Headquarters Company mess tent was a welcome change of scenery.

Both the rain and sky had lightened when I arrived back on top of the hill. Empty brass shells were neatly piled at the tanks; each crew had fired about forty rounds. A rough calculation translated that to be about three-quarters of a ton of HE shells. The tank rounds, mingled with the artillery and mortar shells, had to add up to a hefty amount of tonnage. I could not help wondering what the Chinese morning report would look like. How did their casualty report read?

Kelly grabbed my attention and held me like a magnet. The unpredictability of the day was the focus of my thoughts. Changed plans and diminished expectations had been my reward. A cloud of vapor pouring off the gun tubes was a small token of the unforeseen. And yet adjustments had been made, and the direct-fire support mission had not been interrupted. I had learned a valuable lesson, and I vowed not to get caught in a similar situation again. Now, I thought, what about tomorrow?

A check with both crews showed everything to be in good order except for the ammunition supply—only half a basic load remained in each tank. Morning would be time enough to look after that.

SEVENTEENTH DAY, 0900 HOURS

Morning started out with broken clouds and sunshine—the first we had seen in five days. I had both crews move their cots and bedding out of

Figure 9. Drying out. Sergeant Gardner and Sergeant Davis use a temporary break in the rain to try to dry out soaked clothing and gear. They are using old telephone wire as a clothesline.

the bunkers to air out. The humidity was high, however, so there was not much chance of the items really drying out (figure 9).

Earlier, I had called the Heavy Mortar Company CO, Captain Schwartz, to find out what he knew about plans for the day. Since the critique the previous afternoon, I had not heard a word about the new plan to retake Kelly. He told me that, according to his sources, the next operation was to be a big one. Meanwhile, he said, "we're just shooting H&I at Kelly."[2] He knew nothing beyond the fact that more detailed planning was required, which had delayed the issuing of the Operations order. Our conversation closed with a lot of speculation and unanswered questions regarding our respective roles in the next phase in the fight for Kelly.

Just after 0900 hours Holt called to alert me that First Lieutenant Gus Hinrich, platoon leader, 1st Platoon, Charlie Company, 64th Tank Battalion, had just left the perimeter and was on his way up the hill. I left the bunker, looked down the road, and saw that, sure enough, there was Gus making heavy work of moving uphill. He was alone.

When he got within twenty yards, I shouted: "Good morning, Gus!"

He paused briefly to get his breath. "Hi, Jack! Say, this is one hell of a hill! How are you?"

"Gus, I'm soaking wet. It's nice of you to bring the sunshine. Come over here and sit down." I motioned to my cot.

Gus was a big man. He was in great shape physically, but 350 yards up the hill in the mud had him sucking wind. Our conversation started out with what was happening in the 64th Tank Battalion and more particularly in Charlie Company. I filled him in on the action at Kelly the previous morning and what was expected to take place in the retaking of the outpost. Generally, we confined ourselves to light talk and banter. Finally, I said, "O.K. What's up? You're here for something!" Gus got up from the cot, stepped back a pace, looked down at me, grinned, and then said, "Jack, your turn for R&R has come up. Five days leave in Japan. Barrett sent me here to replace you until you get back." He was smiling at the good news he had just brought me.

I was dumbfounded. This news was totally unexpected. "R&R?"

Well! There it was, right out in the open for everyone to see and hear. As soon as Gus said it I knew exactly what the philosopher meant by the phrase, "Destiny is not a matter of chance, it is a matter of choice." Gus was handing me a ticket, a legitimate ticket off Hill 199. Not all the crossroads in your life are this well marked. And I was clearly at an intersection marked "Go or Stay."

Two main thoughts ran through my head as I sat there composing a response to Gus. This was a chance to get out of this muddy, rain-soaked, grubby, rat-infested, and lethal frontline world. R&R was special because it only came up once in a tour of duty in Korea. The shift from combat to leave was dramatic; in a matter of a few hours you could be at Kimpo Airfield outside of Seoul and then by air get to Japan, muddy combat boots and all. At Camp Drake, outside of Tokyo, you were showered and deloused and issued a class "A" uniform and a five-day pass into the civilized world. All this could happen in a few hours—it was a tempting thought. But then I thought about the 2nd Platoon and my allegiance and responsibilities to five tank crews. The platoon was in the midst of the biggest fight it had ever been in. Could I walk out at this critical juncture in the fight for Kelly? I knew the most intense fighting was still in front of us. I made up my mind.

Gus stood towering over me, his smile beginning to fade a bit. I think he expected me to jump up and tell him I would be packed and ready to go in three minutes. It occurred to me that there might be more to the R&R than was on the surface. Did Barrett think I had reached the end of my string, that my ability to lead was slipping, and was this R&R just a ruse to get me off the hill? No platoon, it was true, had ever been detached from its parent unit for this length of time in the living memory of the 64th Tank Battalion. I dismissed the idea. Captain Barrett would have been here personally to relieve me if he thought I was incapable of leading the platoon. I needed a little more time to answer Gus. I wanted to collect my thoughts and say it just right. After all, the "21" crew was within earshot and had been absorbing the dialog between Gus and me. Stalling for more time, I got up, walked beyond the tank up into the revetment, and looked at Kelly.

Walking back to Gus, I said, "You've made a trip up here for nothing, Gus. I'm going to have to pass on the R&R offer. I belong on this hill; I've got a two-week investment in this place. I led the 2nd Platoon up, and I'm going to lead it down. What's more, there is another assault being planned to retake Kelly, and this platoon will be part of the fire support. I stay with the platoon 'til we come off Hill 199."

The smile on Gus's face had disappeared as I talked. He had been sent here to do a job, and, among other things, I am sure he thought he was doing me a favor. Suddenly the grin on his face reappeared, and he said, "Jack, I told Barrett you would turn down the R&R! I guess you know that there is no way of telling if or when you can be rescheduled for leave."

"Forget the leave, Gus. That's pretty superficial compared to what is going on up here. Believe me, I appreciate Barrett sending you here, and your effort and goodwill, but I'm staying."

Gus lightened up, and with the serious thread of our talk out of the way, he said, "You know, I can drag you off this hill."

And that was certainly true. He could have manhandled me with ease.

"Sure," I smiled, "I know that. But I've two tank crews up here that love a fight. How will you handle that?"

With that exchange, he smiled and departed. I watched him work his way down the hill. When he reached the curve, he waved and then was

gone. A short time later the sky clouded over, and then the rain began
again.

SEVENTEENTH DAY, 1500 HOURS

The Operations order for the next assault on Kelly was handed out in
the 2nd Battalion mess tent. It was indeed to be a large undertaking. You
did not even have to read the Operations order; the size of the gathering
was a clue to the scale of the intended attack. The tent was full. Unit
representation was comprehensive: 15th Infantry regimental staff and
officers of the 1st Battalion and 2nd Battalion, 15th Infantry, were present. There were personnel representing the artillery, and me, representing the tanks. Combat service support made up the rest of the gathering:
engineering, signal, medical, transportation, quartermaster, and ordnance. This was going to be a large-scale attack. The imprint of the 3rd
Division planning was apparent from the introductory remarks made by
members of the division staff. The directive of the I Corps commander,
"Kelly will be retaken!" was highlighted.[3] Mission failure was not an
option.

The 15th Infantry regimental staff presented the details of the operation. It was a simple plan, complicated only in the coordination it would
take to make it all happen on schedule. Weather would play a critical
role in influencing the timely movement of troops. To achieve timely
movement, planners had padded the schedule of events with ample time
to execute maneuvers. I was reminded of something Karl von Clausewitz
had once said: "In war everything is simple, but that which is simple is
difficult." The main thrust of the assault was to retake and hold Kelly. A
subordinate attack on Hill 164 was to protect the flank of Kelly from
Chinese counterattack. The 1st Battalion, 15th Infantry, presently in
regimental reserve, would pass through the MLR held by the 2nd Battalion. Passage through the MLR would commence at 0430 hours, and
the 1st Battalion would be in assault formation at the IP and attack at
0730 hours. Company A would attack Hill 164 west of Kelly, and Company B would attack Kelly. Company C would be 1st Battalion reserve.
A 3rd Division artillery preparation on Hill 164 and Kelly would commence at 0720 hours for a period of ten minutes. After this period, nor-

mal artillery support would begin. Coordinating an assault on this scale required a myriad of details to be completely understood and integrated. The movement of the 1st Battalion from their reserve positions to the 2nd Battalion assembly area was a challenge. Guides were to be provided from the 2nd Battalion to lead 1st Battalion troops to the MLR and then through the safe lanes in the minefields in front of the MLR to the IP. KSCs were to follow the combat units with supplies and litters. And all this maneuvering was to be done under cover of darkness and in the rain. Instructions were given to the artillery, mortar, and tank elements. My initial task was to smoke Hill 317 with WP to obscure Chinese observation of our attacking units and then to shift to HE on Kelly to support Baker Company. The presenters emphasized that the Chinese appeared to be determined to occupy and hold Kelly and could be expected to resist our assault strongly.

The 3rd Infantry Division really wanted Outpost Kelly back in our hands. The size of the assault force and the supporting-fire plan was the equivalent to hitting a fly with a sledgehammer. At least at the moment that is how it seemed. More to the point, I thought, was, how will an infantry battalion execute this plan successfully with the handicap of monsoon rains?

At the conclusion of the meeting, I had an opportunity to renew acquaintance with some of the officers I knew in the 1st Battalion, 15th Infantry. First Lieutenant Alfred De Lorimer, communications officer, and I had served together in the 30th Tank Battalion, Fort Knox, Kentucky. I had met other officers in the battalion last February during Operation Snare. Meeting the 1st Battalion officers today was like old home week without the festive atmosphere. We were all conscious of the serious work that would be afoot the next day.

My request to the S-4, 2nd Battalion, for KSC support fell on sympathetic ears, but he could not assist me. I needed help to resupply the tanks on the hill with ammunition. As he explained, the KSCs committed to him were already fully employed in meeting responsibilities related to supporting both the 1st and 2nd battalions, 15th Infantry. He could not even resupply the Heavy Mortar Company. I was on my own and left to my own resources.

I returned to the tank perimeter and explained the new attack plan to Holt and the three crews. The size of the assault force and the fire plan made a strong impression on everyone. Ever since the failed attack on the twenty-ninth of July, I had been reviewing the role of the tanks and how our effectiveness could be improved. One thing was sure—we would anticipate the steaming gun tubes. The other problem to be overcome was the slow rate of fire due to having to pull stowed rounds from the ammunition wells. My solution for this obstacle was to create a human conveyor belt, a "bucket brigade," that would pass rounds stowed like firewood on the back deck of the tank forward to the loader. Two crewmen outside the tank, standing at the back deck and the loader's hatch, would pick up rounds stowed on the rear deck and pass them through the hatch to the loader. Loading the gun would then be the least time-consuming factor in the firing cycle. With this method, the time involved in adjusting the gun for each indirect-fire shot by the gunner would be the time-consuming factor. A well-trained gunner should be able to get three, possibly four, shots away per minute. Direct fire using the gun's telescope would produce an even faster rate of fire. I had never used this technique before, so there was the element of the unknown. There was also the element of risk. The ammunition, stowed on the back of the tank, would be vulnerable to hostile fire. I decided that there were more advantages than disadvantages.

Support of the assaulting infantry demanded a fast rate of fire. Using the experience of the failed assault as a guide, I estimated that I needed fifty rounds for each tank on the hill. To save steps I elected to use the ammunition presently stowed in the three tanks in the perimeter. The 2nd Battalion ammunition dump was about five hundred yards away, and getting transportation to haul the ammunition to the foot of Hill 199 was next to impossible. I would need all the WP rounds on hand; the remainder would be HE—one hundred rounds in all. I instructed Sergeant First Class Holt to organize the resupply effort. With twenty-five men in the platoon, each man making four trips, on or about one hundred rounds would be brought up the hill. The task was daunting. To begin with, a 90m/m round weighs forty-four pounds. Then, the road up the hill was a mire of ankle-deep mud that was 350 yards long. Above all, the men would have to handle the rounds carefully to avoid creating a dent in the brass shell case. If the shell case was badly dented, a round could jam entering the gun breech and make the gun inoperative until cleared. Clearing jams was typically a difficult and time-consuming procedure.

Well, there it was—a physical task of substantial proportions. I left the details of the resupply effort to Holt. As my contribution to the effort, I carried a WP round to the "21" tank when I left the perimeter. Mounting the hill was a strength-sapping, mind-numbing effort. Later, in the dark, this road would be a real challenge.

In my bunker I briefed the two crews on the hill. First, I covered the assault plan, with emphasis on the role of the tanks and the "bucket brigade" method for rapid firing. I then discussed the immediate task of ammunition resupply and the careful attention that needed to be paid to stowage on the back deck of the tanks. Finally, I had the crews report to Sergeant First Class Holt.

Ingenuity made short work of the resupply effort. Holt had one of the tanks back up the road to just below the washed-out section, which cut the walking distance to less than half. From that point, every round, except shot and hypershot, was removed and carried up the hill. Those antitank, armor-defeating, solid-shot rounds and the very high velocity antitank hypershot rounds would play no role in the coming conflict. Then he did it again with one of the other tanks. The "21" and "22" tanks now had a bit more than a basic load, and we had seventeen WP rounds on hand. I must add that the road was a churned-up mess. This had been grinding work, but everyone knew the significance of each round in supporting the coming attack.

I asked myself what more had to be done. What had I forgotten to do or anticipate? A day ago the surprise had been steam pouring off a hot gun barrel. What will tomorrow's surprise be? I wondered.

I directed both crews to turn in early to be as well rested as possible for the next day. The unexpected was always with us, and a clear mind is an asset in an emergency. It was around 2200 hours then, and we were to be up at 0430 hours. Before turning in, I took the time to reread a letter from my wife, Loel. The letter related mostly to the ordinary, everyday events taking place in Kankakee, Illinois. A quick mental calculation indicated I would have enough points to rotate back to the States in September—only about a month away. Tomorrow would be the thirty-first of July.

EIGHTEENTH DAY, 0430 HOURS

I believed the platoon to be as well prepared for combat as a conscious, deliberate effort could make it. There had been occasions in the past when the platoon became involved in fighting almost without trying. One minute you were detached and uninvolved, and the next minute you were fighting for your life—like the night firefight at Mago-Ri. Today was going to be very different. The entire operation for the retaking of Kelly was highly orchestrated. The scheduling and cueing of the supporting fires, for instance, could only be realized with infinite attention to detail. The role of the tanks was but one element of many contributing to the overall operation. The platoon was a cog in a machine made up of thousands of parts created to achieve a goal—to conquer a hill.

The men had checked and double-checked the tanks for maintenance and operational features. They had checked the ammunition once again for secure storage on the deck of the tanks. Both crews had been instructed on the fire plan. We had reviewed how we would "smoke" the top of Hill 317. They knew why I wanted the gunners to establish their range cards before the cannon barrels started steaming. The crewmen had been cued to when I expected the tempo of our fire on Kelly to increase and how I wanted the loaders and ammunition handlers spelled at their tasks due to the heavy physical effort. I made sure that everyone had washed, shaved, eaten breakfast, and used the latrine. We had been up and about for more than two hours. The last thing I wanted today was a surprise.

I was leaning heavily on the troop-leading training I had received with School Troops, the Armored Center, Fort Knox. At the time I was a platoon leader in the 30th Heavy Tank Battalion, an element of the School Troops. Colonel Joe Fickett, commanding officer of School Troops, conducted the classes personally. During World War II Colonel Fickett had led the reconnaissance battalion that was the "eyes" for

General George S. Patton's 3rd Army as it advanced through France and Germany. One thing that Colonel Fickett had driven home was the "Five P's"—Prior Planning Prevents Poor Performance. How well had I planned for this morning?

By 0700 hours the rain had slackened to a steady downpour. The two crews left the shelter of the bunkers and mounted the tanks; the engines started up with a roar. The knot in my stomach relaxed a little bit, and I opened up the radio net. I heard no unnecessary conversation, just acknowledgment that all parties were on the air—including Holt and the three tanks at the foot of the hill. At 0715 hours I planned to move into the revetments so we could observe the opening guns for the assault on Outpost Kelly. The ten-minute preparatory fires were to commence with a 3rd Infantry Division artillery "time on target" (TOT) at 0720 hours. A TOT is a timed firing in which the shell trajectory from each artillery piece, far or near to the target, is calculated so that the explosive shells arrive at the target simultaneously. In this case, the target was Kelly, and the calculated time for simultaneous arrival was 0720. Subsequent to the TOT, the artillery batteries would return to independent firing for the remaining ten minutes. We did not often get a chance to witness an event like this, and I certainly was not going to miss it.

Over the radio net I ordered the tanks into their revetments. The "21" tank rose up the slight grade and eased into its space. Through the rain I could clearly make out Kelly as a hill, but all detail on the hill was lost in a muddy gray that merged with a gray, overcast sky. The telephone conference call net was scheduled to open at 0715 to confirm that all assault and combat support units were linked together. Actually, the net had been in operation since the 1st Battalion had moved through the MLR at 0430 hours. This 0715 roster check just ensured that all parties were on the hardwire line. While performing these administrative functions, I became conscious that something was amiss. As this sense of something being wrong broke over me, the radio net opened with the call, "This is Two-Two, this is Two-Two. I'm hung up! I can't get into the revetment!" I realized, then, that my sense of something wrong was related to a lack of movement of the "22" tank.

"Roger on that, Two-Two." I thought about this unexpected problem for a brief moment. "I'm sending Davis over to get the details. Stay in

ie net." I did not want to tie up the radio net with detailed explana-
ons. Sergeant Davis would assess the situation and report back to me.

Damn it! It was almost time for the TOT, shortly thereafter my tanks
were to commence "smoking" Hill 317, and it seemed I had a tank that
could not bring its gun to bear on Kelly. Maybe it was not as bad as it
sounded—but I sure had not planned on this.

~

The 1st Battalion, 15th Infantry Regiment, was in place on the MLR
at 0430 hours and started moving through the safe lanes in the barbwire
defenses. The troops had experienced a difficult morning, but at this
point the battalion was on schedule and in forward motion. Earlier,
there had been a lot of "hurry up and wait."

Reveille had been at 0200 hours for the battalion. Roll call was made
on muddy company streets, and the drenched platoon tents sagged as
the rain bore down on them. Everyone was clothed in ponchos and steel
helmets. The battalion was in regimental reserve and located close to
the regimental headquarters. Five days ago, 26 July 1952, the 15th Infantry Regiment had assembled the 1st and 2nd battalions at Camp
Casey in preparation to relieve the 7th Infantry Regiment and take responsibility for the left flank of the 3rd Infantry Division. The 3rd Battalion, in a blocking position behind the 65th Infantry Regiment, would
join the regiment at the MLR on the twenty-seventh. The weather had
been clear and dry. From the fourteenth of July to the twenty-fifth, the
regiment, less the 3rd Battalion, had been in I Corps reserve, with all
units continuing their training and rebuilding their personnel strength.[4]
The regiment was very near to full strength. The relief of the 7th Infantry had taken place over the twenty-seventh and twenty-eighth of July
with only a few minor hitches that were amplified by the effect of monsoon rain. No sooner was the 15th Infantry Regiment settled into its
new surroundings than the Chinese came calling and Outpost Kelly was
lost. And now the chess game continued. Kelly must be retaken as directed by the I Corps Commander.

As the troops moved through the breakfast chow line they found a C
ration display as the last entrée. It was lunch, and the troops had their
choice of meals they would place in their pockets for later in the day.
Canned frankfurters and beans were a popular selection, as were the

hard chocolate bars. Also at the end of the chow line were boxes of extra bandoleers of rifle ammunition. This was an optional choice—you could take what you wanted or not. No rifleman left the mess tent without a full canteen of water; a sergeant stood at the exit and shook each canteen as the men left the tent to ensure the individual water ration was on hand. Church call was held at the 1st Battalion Headquarters area in a tent next to the CP fifteen minutes before the lead truck pulled out.

Squad leaders and platoon sergeants lined their troops up for one more head count before embarking on the waiting two-and-one-half-ton trucks. There would be two trucks to a platoon. Only about half the trucks had tarpaulin covers protecting the cargo area—if you were lucky you got out of the rain temporarily. Coping with confusion was a major leadership problem. The truck drivers had been instructed to deliver their cargo of troops to a specific assembly area to the rear of the MLR. It was up to the platoon leaders and platoon sergeants to get their platoons on the correct trucks. Failing to do this would result in mass confusion at the assembly area because it was here that 2nd Battalion guides were waiting to take the 1st Battalion troops to their designated jumping-off spot on the MLR. The opportunity to make mistakes was lurking in the darkness and in the rain and mud. It was imperative that A Company did not end up in the C Company or B Company assembly area because it would create a time-consuming muddle to unravel. The motor march from the reserve area to the assembly areas was only about a four-mile drive, but the pace made it seem like a long journey. It was stop and go, with only the night-driving lights of the trucks to show the way. Bumped and jostled in the cargo space of the truck, the troops were mostly wrapped up in their own thoughts. Many were new replacements to the 1st Battalion and were experiencing the process of going into battle for the first time. The training exercises at Camp Casey had been designed to develop a sense of teamwork. The exercises dealt first with the offensive squad problems and second with the company-size field exercises. Intermingled were the demonstrations and practical work by assault teams in the attack on bunkers.[5] Now it was 0300 hours, and a convoy of trucks was taking the troops, new and old, to the real thing. Most of the men were wondering how well they would handle whatever was coming at them.

During the tactical briefing at the platoon level the previous evening, the experienced squad and platoon sergeants had stressed the problem of disabled rifles and how to accommodate it. The closest example of the problem was as near as the failed platoon assault by F Company on the morning of the twenty-ninth of July. Rifles fouled with mud in the actions and the muzzles were useless implements and had to be replaced in the middle of the attempted assault on Kelly. KSCs had to bring clean weapons forward so the attack could resume. Those fouled guns had been a hard lesson. Somehow the rifles had to be protected from becoming fouled while the men crawled through the mud. A thin plastic case that slipped over the entire rifle had been issued to protect the guns, but it had two limiting features. First, the plastic was fragile and thus easily torn. Second, the rifle sling was unusable when covered by the plastic case. A rifleman had to be able to sling his rifle over his shoulder to free his hands for other chores, such as carrying ammunition boxes and similar supplies. Other expedients were recommended. The men could place a sock or condom over the muzzle to prevent mud from entering. They could also wrap and tie a towel over the action. In any event, the fouling problem was serious and had to be addressed. This was one more factor for the troops in the trucks to mull over as they approached their assembly areas: will my equipment support me?

At the assembly area the troops disembarked, slipping and sliding in the churned, greaselike mud and went into platoon formations. Another head count was taken. Guides from the 7th Infantry now took over and led the platoons, in a column of twos, up the muddy trails to the MLR. Later, guides would lead the KSCs, with their burdens, forward to follow the assaulting forces. In the dark, on these trails, and in the mud, a column of twos was the only realistic formation to negotiate the foot march. At times the column was reduced to single file. In spite of the prior planning, there was confusion as guides lost their way, which led to marching and countermarching until finally all elements of the 1st Battalion were in place on the MLR. Thanks to the generous timetable in the assault plan, the 1st Battalion had arrived at its jumping-off locations in a timely manner. The time was just a few minutes before 0430 hours. Extra hand grenades were distributed to the waiting riflemen. The 1st Battalion CP was set up on the MLR. Lieutenant Colonel Mills G. Hatfield, CO, 1st Battalion, had selected a G Company bunker that had a good view of both Kelly and Hill 164.

On schedule, the 1st Battalion started its move forward. From the MLR to the IP was eight hundred yards of open ground under observation by the Chinese, which is why this phase of the battalion maneuver was being made under the cover of darkness. Moving through the safe lanes in the barbwire defenses and minefields in front of the MLR was a slow process due to the limited number of lanes. These lanes were narrow and laid out in a zigzagged pattern, but were well marked with white engineer tape to show the edges of the lane. Getting off the safe lane and into a minefield could be a mind-chilling nightmare or worse. The assault positions on the IP for A and B companies were on the flat valley floor close to the base of the hills they were to assault. C Company, in reserve, was in line with the other two companies on the right flank. The last units of the 1st Battalion found their way onto the assault line at 0615 hours. There was plenty of time to make last-minute equipment checks and to get the troops properly deployed. Movement and noise were held to a minimum to avoid detection by the Chinese. Although dawn had come sometime earlier, visibility was impaired due to the rain and dark, overcast sky.

The 1st Battalion, three line companies in the assault, six hundred men, waited for the preparatory fires to begin. It was 0645 hours.

EIGHTEENTH DAY, 0730 HOURS

My wait for Sergeant Davis's return was a mixture of hope and frustration: hope that the hung-up tank could be quickly put back in operation, and frustration that my plans were in jeopardy before a shot had been fired. I turned my attention to the coming TOT.

At 0720 hours, Kelly seemed to erupt like a volcano. Shells smashed into the top and slopes of the hill. Airbursts added to the havoc below. The roar of the explosions, modulated by the rain, initially came in waves. Then the sound settled down to a continuous roll of thunder. Not even the tank engine could mask or cover the sound coming from that churning, dirty-gray mass of explosions enveloping Kelly. I turned my binoculars to the left, to Hill 164, and saw the same scene—a storm of explosions. The artillery preparation would continue for another ten minutes. Could anyone live through this? I wondered.

Davis returned and stood next to the turret on the side pockets and shouted, "They've peeled the left track. The center guides have slipped out of the front three road wheels, and the left rear belly is resting on the ground. The hardstand the tank is resting on has partly washed away—the tank is hung up!"

Damn! This was a worst-case scenario. The disabled tank would not be fixed quickly. My immediate estimate was that the repair would take at least three hours, if not more. It was out of action. The tank could not bring its gun to bear on the target. My five-tank platoon was now down to one tank, fit and in position, to engage the enemy. All the planning and preparation had been nullified by a hardstand that was softened and then washed away by incessant rain. Was it bad luck, or was it a lack of foresight to anticipate this event? I did not have time to do a Monday-morning quarterback analysis. I had three operational tanks at the foot of the hill and no way to get a single one of them to replace the "22" tank. With the road washed out, there was no way to get a tank up the hill. Even if I could get a tank up here, there was no place to put it; the "22" tank blocked that position, and there was no other prepared position. The thought did occur to me that this had to be the ultimate change in plans and diminished expectations. I had Davis stand by while I wrestled with this new dilemma. The solution was pretty obvious. My direct-support mission had not changed; only the number of tanks to do the job had changed. By increasing the rate of fire of the one remaining tank, I could try to compensate for the disabled tank. Accordingly, I opened the radio net and told the "22" tank, with Holt monitoring the instructions, to start getting the track back on and to provide manpower assistance to Davis in moving his ammunition to the "21" tank. The first priority was the ammunition. I told Davis to get a work party together and begin the transfer process but to bring over the WP rounds first. Before he started his task, I had him shut down the "21' tank engine and switch to our "Little Joe" auxiliary engine for electrical power.

There was very little voice traffic on the telephone conference call net as 0730 hours approached. I switched to the tank intercom and told Gardner that the "22" was disabled and that the "21" tank was to carry the full fire mission. The prearranged fire plan called for smoking Kelly with our opening shot to set the range card for that target, then to shift to Hill 317 for the remainder of our WP rounds. There was no specific target on Hill 317 to be blinded by the WP; a specific observation post had not been located. My goal was to blanket the hill with the expectation that somehow some smoke would obscure the visibility of the Chinese. For a moment my thoughts shifted to the "22" tank and the task the men faced. Repairing track is physically tough, knuckle-busting work accomplished with track jacks, pry bars, sledgehammers, and a lot of profanity. When the men are working in rain and mud, the degree of difficulty goes up exponentially. The "22" tank was in for one hell of a morning.

A voice over the phone line shouted, "0730 hours!" On the tank intercom I said, "Gardner, you can fire at will!" The cloud of the WP burst on Kelly was easily distinguished from the artillery and mortar fire hitting the hill—Gardner was right on. His shot had been made visually through the cannon telescope. He quickly made his gunners quadrant adjustment and was all set for indirect fire on Kelly when he finished smoking Hill 317. With his next round he set his range card for Hill 317. One WP round of the seventeen on hand was put aside in the ready rack for unforeseen circumstances. Fifteen rounds were fired very deliberately at Hill 317—about two to three a minute. At round six the steam off the gun tube was enough to prevent Gardner from using the telescope. The wind was coming out of the northeast, but it could not eliminate the steam. The plan was to smoke the upper third of the hill, a strategy that, it was believed, would cover the most likely observation posts. As the firing progressed I noted that the smoke cloud we were trying to create was being dissipated by the wind that was blowing. Chinese observation would not be obscured very long at this rate, I thought. From inside the turret, on the telephone party line, I monitored the progress of the assault. There was a lot of chatter.

Both of the assaulting companies moved forward on schedule. Gardner fired the last round of WP and shifted to Kelly, his new target. The artillery fire on the hill slackened a bit as the 39th Field Artillery became the primary source of covering fire. Our tank fire was lost in the havoc of the artillery and mortar fire crashing into the hilltop. We were delivering two to three rounds a minute now; the "bucket brigade" was working well. The crewmen outside the tank had stuffed their ears with cotton and were wearing their goggles to protect themselves from the concussive wave of the muzzle blast. The cannon muzzle brake, designed to help counter gun recoil, sent a powerful rush of deflected blast rearward. Our fire plan included spelling these men and the loader at frequent intervals. Sustained fire placed a heavy workload on the men. Manhandling forty-four-pound HE rounds in the hot, sweaty confines of a tank turret is a chore. When you couple this with throwing out empty, hot brass shell cases cluttering the fighting compartment floor, you have a recipe for an aching back.

On the phone, both A and B companies reported difficulty in making uphill progress due to the mud and rain. At this stage neither infantry company had met resistance. Then over the telephone came the sound of explosions and the voice of Captain Robert E. Fowler: "This is Baker Company—we're taking incoming! I say again, it's incoming!" This was the first indication the Chinese were going to make a fight for Kelly. There was no sign of resistance yet at Hill 164. The dialogue over the phone was sporadic, and the sound of explosions piled one on the other. The advance up the slope of Kelly continued. A request came over the telephone conference call net to adjust our mortar fire to the north slope; the FO would do the same over the radio to adjust our artillery fire. We must be getting close to the crest of Kelly, I thought. A similar request came from A Company. The specter of casualties due to a "short" round from friendly fire called for a prudent lifting of the mortar and artillery fire from the crest of the two hills to an area farther north.

There was no sign yet that the enemy was still on either hill. Perhaps the preparatory fires had been enough to drive the Chinese out of the entrenchments. Then again, the Chinese had two days to dig in—they were notoriously industrious. I told Gardner over the intercom that the "21" tank was the only gun in the 3rd Division that was now hitting the top of Kelly, and I instructed him to try to increase his rate of fire. I expected that he could manage three to four rounds per minute. His target was the hilltop, but nothing more specific than that, and I wondered whether our shells were hurting the Chinese. At a minimum our fire would make them keep their heads down. At sixteen hundred yards the accuracy of the 90m/m tank gun would permit the advancing riflemen to get very close the top of the hill before I would have to stop firing.

I was intent on listening to the telephone conference call net when Gardner broke in on the intercom and said, "I've got a good visual picture in the 'scope'! The steam is gone." This message brought me up sharp. Preoccupied with monitoring the intercom with one ear to the headset and the other ear to the telephone, I had failed to notice that the rain had stopped! I popped up waist high out of the turret and looked at the gun barrel. There was no steam—just a slight wavy heat mirage. And the wind was now hitting us from the east.

"How much detail can you see?" I asked.

"I can see a lot of things on that hill now," he responded.

"O.K. Go to visual. The infantry is pretty far up the slope, so pick up the rate of fire. How about five or six rounds a minute?"

"Can do, sir," he replied.

This event seemed just short of a miracle. In any case, something was going our way for a change.

It flashed through my mind that his response was very appropriate. It was the motto of the 15th Infantry Regiment: "Can Do." That regiment had a long history, starting in 1798 with its participation in many of our country's wars. The pidgin English motto "Can Do" symbolized the service of the 15th Infantry Regiment from 1912 to 1938 in Tientsin, China, when it protected civilians during the Chinese revolution.

I looked at my watch—we had been in action for less than half an hour. I scanned Kelly with my binoculars to see whether I could detect any movement of our assault force. I did not see any movement, but as Gardner had indicated, there was a lot to see on the hilltop. On Hill 199 we were about one hundred feet higher in elevation than Kelly; we were shooting downhill. The sky had brightened appreciably when the rain stopped, and details such as the outline of trenches were clearly visible. As occurred two days ago, I could find no orange signal panel. The telephone conference call net was crowded with a lot of talk.

A hurried voice, First Lieutenant Woodrow F. Woods, CO, A Company, recently assigned to the unit from D Company, dominated the conference call net.[6] "We've got the top of 164. There were no Chinese here to stop us. Able Company is digging in, and we can use those KSCs now."

Then another voice spoke: "My first platoon is taking automatic-weapons fire from Kelly; it's coming into our right flank!" It was Captain Robert E. Fowler speaking. I thought the situation was developing quickly. We had secured Hill 164, but Kelly remained in Chinese hands. Despite the artillery and mortar preparation, the Chinese had elected to stand and make a fight of it.

"Gardner, put two rounds on the right flank of the south trench. Can you see it? The infantry are taking automatic-weapons fire." I was beginning to get adept at juggling the intercom headset and the telephone handset.

"Yes, sir," he replied as the gun tube swung to the right.

I watched the rounds strike and then said, "O.K. Now put two into the left flank of that trench." I did not know whether there was a machine gun there, but it would be a likely location. The gun swung left, and the rounds hit in quick succession. The outline of the trench was not perfectly clear, but what could be seen permitted a good guess as to where the rest of the trench was located. Gardner resumed firing at the few features he could distinguish on the hill. On the telephone line the dialogue indicated that B Company was no longer taking automatic-weapons fire.

Shortly after Gardner began his search for targets on the hill, a tremendous explosion erupted on Kelly. A large black cloud and debris flew hundreds of feet in the air.

"Gardner, what was that?" I asked, flabbergasted.

"Sir, I don't know. Our fuses are still set on 'super quick.' We just got some sort of secondary effect. Something on that hill just let go high order!"

I broke into the conference call net conversation and said, "This is Tanks. We just got a huge secondary explosion on Kelly. Did we have anything stored up there that would blow like that?"

There was a pause, and then the S-3, 2nd Battalion, said, "Has to be Chinese. We never had anything up there that would explode like that."

The "21" tank had probably by accident struck a Chinese cache of grenades or antipersonnel mines, and it resulted in a high-order explosion.

I continued, "I can't see any movement of our troops. Are we getting close to the top? Do you want me to cease fire?"

"This is Baker Company," the CO broke in. "Keep firing—we'll tell you when to stop."

"This is Tanks," I said. "Roger, out!" I still did not know how close the riflemen were to the crest of Kelly. They must be far enough down the slope not to be too concerned by the 90m/m projectiles whizzing over their heads and striking the top of Kelly. If the infantry were downslope one hundred yards from the crest, the trajectory of my 90m/m rounds would be about sixty feet over their heads.

"We're getting small-arms and automatic-weapons fire now!" It was Captain Fowler, B Company, again. Through my binoculars I still could not make out any movement. My guess was that the lead platoon was stalled within a hundred yards or less from the south trench and was taking the brunt of the Chinese defensive actions. Farther down the slope the other platoons would be making their way forward. I wondered to myself how many of the rifles being dragged up that hill would be serviceable when B Company got to the top.

I broke into the telephone conference call net and said, "This is Tanks. I'm going to place HE into the trench. You'll have to tell me when to stop. Over."

The S-3, 2nd Battalion, responded, "Roger on that, Tanks. Go ahead. Out."

On the intercom I said, "Gardner, our infantry are taking small-arms and machine-gun fire. I want you to work over the south trench. There are Chinks in there. Sweep the length of the trench from left to right, then right to left. Use a ten-mil adjustment between bursts. Fire as fast as you can. I'll tell you when to stop."

In artillery terms, a "mil" is an expression of angular measurement; there are 6,400 mils to a circle. At a distance of one thousand yards, the chord of an arc of one mil would span one yard in width. At sixteen hundred yards, with someone using a ten-mil adjustment, each burst would explode sixteen yards from the previous burst. I calculated roughly that five rounds would sweep the trench in one direction. With mathematical precision, Gardner commenced to place HE shells into the trench. Our rate of fire had to be six to eight rounds a minute at this stage. How many sweeps had been made? Was this the third or fourth sweep? What would that come to—twenty-five rounds? The roar of the muzzle blast from the "21" tank was now continuous.

No living thing can stand up to this, I thought. If the Chinese stay in that trench, they will be shredded.

Engaging the trench was defined in the military textbooks as a "target of opportunity." Twenty minutes ago, in the rain, an easily seen target was the furthest thought on my mind. Hitting the top of the hill was the best we could do with indirect-fire technique. Now, as the sky brightened, an unplanned target appeared. It was the ragged outline of a trench full of Chinese—and our 90m/m cannon was pounding the hell out of the enemy.

The wind from the east blew the muzzle-blast smoke clear of the telescope view. Brass shell casings covered the floor of the fighting compartment; we had no time to discard them from the tank. The smell of sweat, hot brass on an oily floor, gunpowder fumes, and rain-drenched clothing mingled inside the turret. I glanced outside the turret to watch the "bucket brigade" working to a steady cadence of passing rounds from the back deck to the loader's hatch and then through the hatch to the waiting arms of the loader. The "21" tank and its crew represented a precision weapon dedicated to destroying the enemy. I put my binoculars on Kelly and watched the rhythmic progression of bursting shells work their way along the dim outline of the trench.

"We're going up!" exclaimed a voice on the telephone conference call net. B Company was moving forward. How close did the infantry intend to get to the crest of Kelly before I would be told to hold my fire? I wondered.

"Lift the tank fire! Lift the tank fire!" The command came as a relief to me because of my mounting concern of a friendly fire incident. "Roger!" I responded. On the intercom I told Gardner to cease firing. Suddenly, the tank became very quiet, with just the soft purr of the auxiliary engine providing a subtle background sound. My watch showed 0810 hours. Forty minutes of almost continuous firing since the infantry crossed the IP at 0730 hours. Have we done enough, have we cleaned out the trench? I wondered. I put my binoculars on Kelly and finally saw some movement. I could make out several men standing on the top of the hill. Kelly was ours! Now all we had to do was hold it.

There was continuous cross talk on the conference call net. On the last rush up the hill, B Company had not received a single round of small-arms fire. They had met no resistance—the Chinese were gone. Now there was an urgent need for the supplies being brought forward by the KSCs. A Chinese counterattack was expected, so preparation for the defense of the newly won hill was a top priority. At least the rain had stopped. My priority was to get the "21" tank ready for a counterattack. I wondered what role the tank would play. A quick inventory of the rounds remaining on the back deck showed a total of thirteen. The fighting compartment was being cleared of empty brass; the "clang" of the cases hitting the pile outside of the tank had a sharp, clear ring. We would make a count later for my after-action report.

I monitored the party line net for another few minutes and concluded that the business at hand dealt mainly with logistics to support Hill 164 and Kelly (figure 10). I turned the monitoring over to Sergeant Davis and called Holt on the SCR-508. I told him that the assault was successful and that the 15th Regiment was going into a defensive posture. I directed that the radio net continue to be monitored, noting that it was 0815 hours.

∼

The riflemen of the three line companies, A, B, and C, of the 1st Battalion, 15th Infantry, were on the IP at 0630 hours and in their assault formations. Prior to moving into the attack, they had witnessed the 3rd Division artillery TOT. They had seen ten minutes of artillery preparation from a vantage point four to five hundred yards from the two hills getting the pounding. Rain dampened some of the sound, but that volume of artillery concentrated on two small hilltops created an impressive noise. To some of the troops it gave heart that the Chinese would withdraw from the hilltops under the weight of the bombardment. To others the spectacle meant that the Chinese would be wide-awake and waiting for the assault force to arrive. At 0730 hours A and B companies crossed the line of departure and moved out toward their objec-

Figure 10. The fight for Outpost Kelly. Lieutenant Siewert, platoon leader, monitors the conference call telephone network while awaiting Chinese counterattack immediately after the retaking of Kelly.

tives; C Company remained in reserve.[7] To many of the troops an assault in daylight was counter to much of their training and actual combat experience. Even though the day was gray and heavily overcast with steady rain, it was still daylight. A sense of being overexposed was prevalent, particularly with Hill 317 only one thousand yards to the left flank of A Company. It was like having the Chinese looking right down your throat.

A Company gained the top of Hill 164 at 0800 hours. The assault was opposed by mortar fire near the base of the hill, but after that point the movement of the force went smoothly up the hill. The real problem was the footing. Riflemen were reduced to crawling at times on hands and knees because better progress was made that way. Standing was awkward due to slipping and sliding in the mud, and a soldier became a better target when he was upright. It was slow progress, but it was steady. The men quickly discovered that a poncho, although an asset in the rain under normal circumstances, became a liability when crawling uphill in the mud, especially when pulling a box of belted machine-gun cartridges and dragging a rifle at the same time. The lower slope of Hill 164 was littered with discarded ponchos.

The FO accompanying A Company shifted the artillery fire striking Hill 164 when the lead platoon reached a point about one hundred yards from the hilltop. It was then that the lead squad began to feel really vulnerable. Up to this point the artillery fire would keep the enemy deep in protective cover, but when the fire lifted they would come out and have a clear downhill shot at the advancing infantry. As it turned out for A Company, the Chinese were not on the hill to oppose the assault force. No one could determine whether the Chinese had occupied the hill when the attack commenced with the ten-minute artillery preparation. What the men did discover, with great relief, was that the Chinese did not wish to contest the advance with a small-arms firefight. As the riflemen moved onto the hilltop, the rain stopped. Work began immediately to construct defenses. Hill 164 was not fortified. The riflemen unbuckled their light combat packs, removed the short-handled collapsible shovels, and set to work digging. The most probable attack by the Chinese would be from the north. First Lieutenant Woods got on the field phone, reported his situation, and requested KSC assistance.

Troop leaders inspected the weapons in the hands of the riflemen and found many to be unserviceable from being dragged through the mud. The troops attempted to clear and clean the guns immediately, but the field conditions made weapon disassembly and cleaning very awkward. Improving the serviceability of the weapons on hand was marginal at best.

A Company had achieved its mission to protect the flank of Kelly; it now faced the probable counterattack by the Chinese.[8] It was now 0815 hours.

On the lower slope of Kelly, B Company encountered the same movement difficulties as experienced by the assault force on Hill 164. Ponchos were discarded, and the advance moved forward at a crouch or a crawl. A mortar barrage struck the company at approximately the same location experienced by the F Company platoon two days earlier. The concentration was of short duration, and the company moved on. Although the rain interfered with ease of maneuver, it also tended to obscure movement. It was this feature that quite likely contributed to the failure of the Chinese to use their mortars and artillery more effectively. The lead platoon of B Company found some small comfort in the fact that they had not come upon a Chinese listening post located on the lower slope of Kelly. It could be an indicator that the Chinese had abandoned Kelly. Another encouraging development was that the rain had stopped.

When the company lead element was about one hundred yards from the south trench, the FO elected to shift the artillery fire from off the hilltop to the north slope and beyond. This move had two immediate effects: it reduced the possibility of a friendly fire incident, and it would provide a zone of fire to interfere with possible Chinese reinforcement to Kelly. Over the telephone conference call net, Captain Fowler requested that the mortars shift their concentrations as well. On the top of the hill, however, shells could still be heard exploding methodically. It was 90m/m tank fire pinpointing features on the top of Kelly. As welcome as this shelling was, there was a disconcerting element to it. A sonic boom accompanied each shot. The riflemen on the hillside heard, just a fraction of a second prior to the explosion on the hilltop, the loud, sharp, cracking report of the supersonic projectile sixty feet overhead. Crack—boom! It took a few rounds to realize that there was no danger. At this stage of the assault, too, the riflemen were feeling the strain of the physical effort to reach the summit of Kelly. The inclination was to take a short rest, a breather. The steepest part of the hill was still before them. The troop leaders knew this was no time to slow down, however. When the artillery and mortars lifted off Kelly, the Chinese, if they were up there, would be out of their holes and into their firing positions. Now was the time to accelerate the advance.

The Chinese were in their firing positions! Automatic-weapons fire came into the right flank of the leading platoon. Sergeant First Class Theodore A. Cook, platoon sergeant and acting platoon leader, 1st Platoon, B Company, was working his way up a finger of the hill to the right of the trail. The footing was better there. He shouted to his men to run for the protection of a small knob, or outcropping, to their immediate front. There was cover and concealment here from the machine-gun fire, and it gave Ted Cook a brief opportunity to assess his situation. Now

Chinese rifle fire could be heard along the trench. Mortar fire slammed into the hill. A quick glance ahead showed Cook another knob a short distance up the slope. With a loud shout, Cook and his platoon rushed as a group to the next protective cover.[9]

Sergeant First Class Cook was not unfamiliar with Kelly as a hill—he had been here before. On 4 February 1952 he had been on the hill, and the outpost platoon he was with had been assaulted by an overwhelming Chinese force. The fight for the hill commenced about noon on a clear winter day and turned into close combat—hand grenades, submachine guns, and pistols. Cook suffered a severe mortar wound to his right thigh, and, alone, he barely made it back to the MLR. The U.S. platoon had been ejected from the hill with heavy losses—three dead and fourteen wounded out of a platoon of twenty-nine riflemen. Now it was five months later. Ted Cook reflected that, again, the Chinese held Outpost Kelly.

The firing from the trench was positive confirmation that the Chinese were going to make a fight for Kelly. Over the phone, Captain Fowler relayed the information of the hostile machine-gun fire his unit was taking. B Company was stalled. As the company lay face down in the mud, tank fire smashed into the trench where the machine-gun fire originated. Automatic fire from the trench ceased.

Shortly, the advance resumed but almost immediately ran into more small-arms and automatic-weapons fire. Again B Company stalled, this time with elements of the company within fifty to seventy-five yards of the south trench. The CO promptly relayed this event over the telephone conference call net. For roughly the next four minutes, B Company watched and heard an uninterrupted series of explosions tear along the south trench—back and forth—with a methodical rhythm. Finally, Captain Fowler directed over the phone that the tank fire cease. B Company moved forward.

The advance was not a grand sweeping maneuver but rather a column of squads clambering up and through the narrow safe lane and broken barbwire defenses along the south trench and then fanning over the hilltop. The men had rifles at the ready and bayonets attached. They held hand grenades, which were ready to be thrown. The assault force was unopposed.

They found no live Chinese. It was a walkover, and Kelly had been retaken.[10]

Sergeant First Class Cook was among the first on the crest, and he surveyed a scene of desolation. The hilltop was pitted with many craters from numerous shells; the trenches in various locations had caved in. By radio and telephone the men gave instructions to stop the friendly mortar and artillery fire. Kelly became a quiet and solemn place. There were no cheers and wild jubilation, just exhausted survivors. They found a very large crater near the center of the hilltop. The south trench and surrounding area near it were in shambles, a grim sight detailing the havoc of 90m/m tank fire. They found no enemy casualties on the hill, only scattered body parts in and around the south trench. This was not unusual. The Chinese attempted to maintain an immaculately clean battle area. Whenever possible the Chinese would carry off their dead and wounded to keep the U.S. forces from assessing how effective their efforts had been. There were accounts of the Chinese policing up a battle area to the extent that all weapons, ammunition, packs, clothing, food, and other gear—even bloody bandages—were removed. The Chinese had disengaged, leaving Kelly in the hands of B Company and leaving the riflemen to wonder also how many had been there and how many escaped or were carried away.

Enemy mortar fire began to hit the hilltop. Was there to be a counterattack? It was certainly a probability, almost a certainty, and now it became the major focus of B Company. The riflemen scrambled to the task of consolidating the defenses of the hilltop. As with most outpost fortifications constructed by the U.S. Army, a circular trench located on the military crest surrounded the top of the hill. This trench was protected, in turn, by barbwire and, occasionally, by an antipersonnel minefield. Military crest entrenchments are on the downslope of the hill or ridge, as opposed to the actual topographical crest, and face the expected approach of the enemy. The approaches to an outpost are from all sides, hence the circular trench around the hilltop. Barbwire was not available; that would have to be brought up by the KSCs. Other supplies, such as shovels and picks, would be needed to augment the personal entrenching tool, the collapsible shovel, carried by the riflemen. Kelly could accommodate a rifle platoon with ease; a full rifle company was a tight fit.

The men needed to do a lot of work to bring Kelly into a defensible condition. The time was 0815 hours.

EIGHTEENTH DAY, 0815 HOURS

With regard to the tanks, we had much to do now that our heavy firing
contribution to the assault was over. The "21" crew performed maintenance and readied the tank for further combat by organizing the fighting compartment. They pulled rounds from the ammunition wells and
placed them in the ready rack. They then counted our empty brass shell
casings—we had fired 109 rounds. The "21" tank had delivered just over
two thousand pounds of projectiles—a ton of high explosives in forty
minutes. That was a lot of firing for a tank crew, and the day was not
over. I told Holt over the radio what was happening and directed that he
shut down the SCR-508 radio; I would get back to him by phone later
as needed. Davis turned off our auxiliary engine, and Hill 199 became
quiet.

The telephone conference call net was still operational and monitored by all units that had been on line since 0430 hours. The traffic
was administrative and logistic in content, so I turned the phone over to
Gardner. I was anxious to see what progress the "22" tank crew was
making in restoring the tank to a serviceable state. When I got there the
crew was in the last stage of getting the track back on. They had to have
been working like beavers to get this far this fast. The effort had required
breaking the track near the idler wheel, resetting the track center guides
into the road wheels by pry bars and digging, and then reconnecting the
track. I watched the track center guides being forced into the gap between the paired road wheels. Later, track jacks would pull the track
shoes together, and the end connectors would be fitted, which would
complete the job. This had been heavy-duty, knuckle-busting, back-
breaking labor by any standard of measure—a track, made up of many
individual shoes, weighs four tons. As I stood watching this process, Sergeant Davis came running up and said, "Sir, you'd better get back on
the telephone. Kelly is taking mortar fire! That counterattack may be
starting."

Davis and I hurried back to the "21" tank. Gardner handed me the telephone when I got to the turret and said, "Kelly is catching it. B Company is asking for the KSCs and fortification stuff. So is A Company." The dull rumble of mortar fire hitting Kelly was quite audible in the stillness on Hill 199. Through the telephone the explosions were very sharp; Captain Fowler had the phone handset locked open so everything that was to be heard, mortars or conversation, was on the conference call net. The conversation had an undercurrent of urgency and desperation. A glance at my watch showed 0840 hours. B Company had been digging in for only about half an hour, not much time to develop useful cover and protection from mortars. More than that, was this the prelude to the expected Chinese counterattack? I wondered. And what role would the tanks play if this was the counterattack? Very limited, I thought, because the top of Kelly will be off-limits, and the tank gun cannot hit the rear or sides of the hill. We could hit only what we could see, the south slope.

A Company broke into the net, "We're taking mortar and small-arms fire. Artillery, too!" First Lieutenant Woods went on to describe a large Chinese force coming from the north and the west. He was concerned about his ability to hold Hill 164 due to the limited number of serviceable rifles.[11]

This was bad news. Is this a two-pronged counterattack? I asked myself as I monitored the conference call net. Are Kelly and Hill 164 to be hit simultaneously? The line was jammed with dialogue, with the infantry on both hills dominating the traffic. I tried to visualize what I was overhearing as I participated silently. Could this be the introduction to another setback much like the one we had two days ago? Do the Chinese have enough strength to strike us in two locations at the same time? B Company indicated no sign of enemy troops, just a continuous mortar bombardment. Now A Company was requesting mortar support to augment the artillery that the A Company FO had placed on the advancing Chinese. With both the U.S. and Chinese forces dropping mortar and artillery shells in the same general location, the sound coming from Hill 164 was imposing. The resistance of our forces, however, was short lived—too few functioning weapons and too many oncoming enemy combatants. Holding Hill 164 was untenable. A Company was instructed to disengage and retire to the MLR. This maneuver introduced a change in the tactical equation facing Kelly. Its west flank was now exposed to a Chinese force, estimated at company strength, which was only six hundred yards away. Meanwhile, Kelly was taking mortar fire and facing the prospect of an imminent Chinese counterattack. The outpost was out on a limb, a fragile limb. I assessed again the role the tanks could play, and again the answer was, "not much." At best, the tanks had the capability of covering a retreat from Kelly by placing fire on the hilltop and then on the south slope in the event the Chinese pursued our riflemen down the hill. This appeared to be my only realistic option, but in my view it was a poor choice.

Monitoring the phone, awaiting events to happen, gave me a moment to think about a request that had been made to the two line companies. It was shortly after the companies had successfully taken Hill 164 and Kelly. They were asked to provide a body count of Chinese dead. Neither company had anything to report. An enormous amount of preparatory fires had been placed on each hill, and yet there was little to show for it. The tank fire had also made a contribution, but the effect had been a torn-up south trench. The after-action report would have to read "No estimate of enemy casualties was made for 31 July 1952," which posed an administrative problem for the 15th Infantry Regiment. Enemy dead body count was an important statistic. It emphasized the importance the UN command placed on a running score of enemy dead. In July 1952 in Korea, the yardsticks for success were holding onto real estate and increasing the enemy dead. On the MLR the enemy dead were called "dead gooks." I called them "dead Chinks." Regardless, it was all of one pattern, a mental subterfuge to avoid thinking of the enemy as human beings. Ambiguous terms are used to dehumanize the people we are killing so that we can more easily rationalize what we are doing, I thought. But you can only fool yourself for so long; sooner or later it catches up with you, I realized. In 1952 the medical term was "battle fatigue"; in modern terms, the medics call it "posttraumatic stress syndrome."

An order was given over the telephone conference call net to C Company, the reserve, to occupy and hold Hill 164. The time was now 0915 hours. This order demonstrated that flank protection for Kelly was important. It would take awhile for the unit to move into the assault position at the foot of Hill 164. Then, over the conference call net, the S-3, 1st Battalion, said, "Tanks, be prepared to place tank fire on Hill 164

Figure 11. The fight for Outpost Kelly. The "21" tank is in hull defilade. Kelly has been retaken. We are awaiting a counterattack by the Chinese. Note the few remaining rounds stacked on the back deck of the tank.

when Charlie Company assaults the hill. Commence your fire when our artillery and mortar fire is lifted."

"This is Tanks. Roger, out!" I responded. The 2nd Platoon was still in the combat action; we still had a contribution to make. With a little luck the "22" tank might get in the fight if the crew could get the track back on in time.

My estimate of the distance to Hill 164 was twelve hundred yards, and our visibility was good because the sky had brightened slightly. I pulled the "21" crew together by the turret and explained the new turn of events and how we would handle our responsibilities. Essentially we would repeat what we had done to support B Company when they had assaulted Kelly. Gardner wanted to know what we were to do about ammunition. I said we would pull rounds from the ammunition wells and stack them on the back deck of the tank. Thirty rounds from the wells should be adequate; we still had thirteen on the deck from our earlier fire mission (figures 11 and 12). Davis started up our auxiliary engine. I

Figure 12. Awaiting a counterattack. High point on the horizon is Hill 317, held by the Chinese; it is about one and one-quarter miles away.

then sent Davis back to the bunker to call Holt and tell him to get back on the radio. When Holt came on the SCR-508 net, I told him of our situation. Everything was done that could be done; we stood by, waiting for the assault to commence.

At Kelly the situation had not changed. The Chinese had not yet made an appearance, but their mortar fire continued. The progress of C Company toward Hill 164 was announced from time to time over the party line. The unit had about one thousand yards to go from their reserve position to Hill 164. As they were maneuvering into their assault formation, I put the "21" tank crew into full ready status. Gardner had his sights on the hilltop, the "bucket brigade" was standing by, and I was monitoring the phone.

Even as C Company was forming at the foot of the hill, a heavy, continuous artillery and mortar barrage struck it. Whether by luck or design, the barrage hit the company squarely where it stood. The effect was devastating—there were many casualties. The company was ordered to withdraw and return to its reserve position and be prepared to reinforce

Kelly. Our artillery and mortars continued to fall on the Chinese at Hill 164, but at the "21" tank we were given no order to fire. I glanced at my watch and saw that it showed 0945 hours. We had experienced a setback, and the tactical situation on Kelly had not been altered. Their flank was still exposed. In the big picture, the 15th Infantry Regiment was waiting for the Chinese counterattack at Kelly. Conference call traffic was now dedicated to the movement of supplies and fortification equipment to Kelly on an expedited basis. After a quarter of an hour, I had the crew stand down but told them to be ready on a moment's notice in case we were needed. I gave Holt the same information, and then I shut down the radio net. I turned the monitoring of the party line over to Davis and walked over to the "22" tank. As I approached that location I could hear the reports of our 4.2-inch mortars sending out another salvo. I was sure they were giving Hill 164 a working over.

The crew had reconnected the left-side track and had placed dunnage at the front of the tracks on both sides of the tank to increase the traction once the vehicle started to move. They had done a lot of digging on the left side as part of the process of getting the track back under the road wheels. They had jammed timbers and other heavy debris into the excavated area for support and better traction. Even though the rain had stopped earlier in the morning, the mud was still deep and greaselike. With the tank hung up the way it was at the left rear, the tank driver was probably going to get only one chance at getting the tank up and out. I remembered when we had that tank belly down in a rice paddy and needed two tanks in tandem, with cables, to pull it free. In the tight confines of the present location, a tow by another tank was not an option. The crew had done everything within its means to make the coming effort a success. I stepped back and watched the final maneuver. The engine was idling steadily. Then the driver revved up the engine, and the tank moved slowly, almost gracefully, up the slight grade and into the revetment. The "22" crew had been at this job for almost three hours; it was now 1015 hours. The crew had been oblivious to the events that had taken place since 0730 hours, so I brought them up to date on the combat situation. I told them to be prepared for a counterattack by the Chinese. I could not be specific about the support we would be expected to provide because I did not know myself how we would be employed. Before leaving, I congratulated all the men. They had under-taken a difficult task and, in relative terms, made short work of it.

When I returned to the "21" area, I discovered that all the gear in the bunker had been removed and was now piled up in disarray outside the structure. Gardner cautioned me not to enter—the bunker was in a progressive state of collapse. I noticed a shift in the column supports at the entrance, and as I watched, I could detect a slow movement down-hill. The "21" crew stood and stared at the slow-moving spectacle. First the outer wall of sandbags slid slowly downhill, and then the roof por-tion of sandbags leisurely collapsed with scarcely a sound. I gave a silent prayer of thanks that the crew and I had witnessed this event from the outside. Several large rats scurried away to find a new home.

Of course, now the crew and I had a new problem—protection from hostile fire. It was too soggy for foxholes, so I directed that we would take shelter, as needed, in the tank. For normal shelter from the elements, we would use our hex tent.

Davis, who was in the turret monitoring the conference call net, called my attention to the smoke rising on the north and west sides of Kelly. It was our mortar fire placing a smoke screen to conceal the forti-fication work in progress on Kelly. Davis said that the enemy mortar fire slowed down around 1030 hours, about the time lead elements of the 2nd Battalion and their KSC work parties arrived with supplies. Water, food, clean rifles, ammunition, litters for the casualties, shovels, barb-wire, and other items were now arriving at the hilltop. It was a long trek from the MLR to the top of Kelly, about fifteen hundred yards. Much of that distance was under the observation of the Chinese. And in the background was the ever-present threat of a Chinese counterattack. The movement of supplies forward and dead and wounded rearward would go on all day.

The two tank crews stayed on station, ready to assume their combat stance quickly if the call came. Crewmen took turns monitoring the conference call net; around 1800 hours it was announced that only spo-radic machine-gun fire and mortars were hitting the hill. The odds that a Chinese counterattack would occur had become small, considering the strength we now had on the hill. Good progress was being made in improving the defenses. The conference call net was closed down with the statement that the 1st Battalion was now in complete control of Outpost Kelly.

~

By 0830 hours the mortars striking Hill 164 had increased in volume, and First Lieutenant Woods, CO of A Company, became convinced his unit was in for a Chinese counterattack. He was primarily concerned about the means he had on hand to repulse the enemy. He expressed his concern over the conference call net and was told that our Heavy Mortar Company was standing by with preplanned concentrations ready at his call. He was told that the KSC work parties, with fortification supplies, would not reach Hill 164 until about 1000 hours. The FO with the company was in contact with the Fire Direction Control Center, 39th Field Artillery, and was prepared to call in artillery concentrations in the event of a Chinese counterattack. The riflemen had bent to the task of developing defenses with their small hand shovels. A weapons inventory for serviceability had been made as soon as the hilltop had been occupied. Many of the rifles were fouled with mud.[12] In the present conditions of mud and enemy mortar fire, field cleaning was a marginal option. Several riflemen were assigned the task of disassembling, cleaning, and reassembling M1 rifles, while the majority of the riflemen did entrenching. It was at this state of readiness that the Chinese infantry hit A Company. Their assault came from the north and the west, with the force estimated to be at company strength. Our mortar and artillery concentration fell on the Chinese advance, but it did not stop them. The Chinese mortars and artillery fell on Hill 164. There were too few functioning weapons to oppose the assault, and A Company was instructed to disengage and return to the MLR. They retired as ordered, taking their dead and wounded with them. To avoid being an attractive target for Chinese artillery, the company dispersed and moved rearward in an infiltrating manner. The hill was lost at 0845 hours.

The west flank of Kelly was now exposed. Hill 164 was being held to provide flank protection so that Kelly could consolidate its defenses in relative security. That goal had been negated by the success of the Chinese attack. B Company now occupied Kelly, but its state of readiness was no better than that of A Company. Restoration of flank protection by holding Hill 164 with friendly forces was mandatory.

Accordingly, First Lieutenant Eugene V. Gaetzke, CO, C Company, was alerted to reoccupy Hill 164. He had joined C Company on 21 July 1952 and had just been appointed commanding officer.[13] In its reserve location the company organized for a foot march to the hill, a distance of about one thousand yards. The order to move out came at 0915 hours. All the rifleman in the company knew that the Chinese would observe their advance. It was an uncomfortable thought. Movement along the flat valley floor was impeded by the muddy conditions, and as a consequence the tail end of the strung-out company column did not arrive at the assault formation area until 1000 hours.

The relatively flat terrain at the base of Hill 164 was well suited to organizing the assault formation. Before the final arrangements were made, however, the Chinese unloaded a heavy artillery and mortar barrage on the assembly area. It was close to being a direct hit. The assault formation was stopped dead in its tracks even before the tail of the column had arrived. Riflemen who were readying for an assault were thrown into confusion and panic. The barrage continued, and men dispersed in all directions. Unit cohesion was lost, and troop leaders at all levels were left with scattered squads and platoons. Casualties mounted. Amid the explosions, First Lieutenant Gaetzke described his situation over the telephone conference call line and was told to reorganize, return to his reserve location, and await further orders. Reorganizing was difficult with stragglers to the four winds; men were unable to find their platoon, and frustrated platoon leaders and platoon sergeants were unable to find their men. Command and control had been badly disrupted. The disorganized company moved back along the trail they had just come up, bringing their dead and wounded with them. Order was restored as the company moved toward the reserve area, but many of the men were still not with their correct squad when the company arrived in the reserve location. It was here that the company was fully brought to good order and a head count was made. The casualties, dead and wounded, were sent back to the MLR. C Company was told to be prepared to reinforce Kelly in the event of a counterattack by the Chinese.

Captain Fowler had a big task in front of him—fortifying Kelly. The artillery and mortar fire bombardment and the tank cannon fire had made a shambles of the previous entrenchments. Moreover, he faced the prospect of establishing a fortification for an entire company of infantry. The previous arrangement had been designed to accommodate a rifle platoon. The muddy conditions on Kelly made entrenching difficult. At best the riflemen could dig an individual foxhole, but only with great difficulty because the sloppy mud would cave in repeatedly. Rebuilding these trenches with a small shovel was an exercise in futility, but the riflemen tried. Digging was the only salvation from the continuous incoming mortar fire placed on Kelly by the Chinese. It was around 1030 hours that the first element of the 2nd Battalion, escorting the heavily burdened KSC work parties, arrived to assist in improving the defenses.[14] These work parties, and the supplies they brought, were welcome indeed. The items they brought consisted of clean weapons, ammunition, food, water, shovels, barbwire, and other fortification supplies. To obscure the hilltop from the observation of the Chinese, men in the friendly 4.2-inch mortar company placed a WP smoke screen on the north and the west slopes of Kelly. It worked. Enemy fire, mortars and machine guns, became sporadic and finally died away late in the day. All afternoon the KSC work parties arrived with supplies. Some of the KSCs stayed to assist with the rebuilding of the trenches and barbwire obstacles, and others carried litters of wounded men back to the MLR. The wounded were then taken to the 2nd Battalion medical aid station.

By 1800 hours the defenses were greatly improved, and there had been no evidence of a ground attack being launched by the Chinese. B Company, 1st Battalion, 15th Infantry Regiment, occupied and held Outpost Kelly.

Captain Charles D. Neilson, CO, G Company, 2nd Battalion, had been directed earlier to relieve B Company during the hours of darkness on 31 July 1952. Accordingly, at 2000 hours Captain Neilson and his entire company approached the safe lane leading to the crest of Kelly. A short while later the relief took place, and Captain Fowler led B Company down the hill and back to the MLR.

By 2100 hours all three companies of the 1st Battalion had returned to the MLR. A Company had returned earlier in the day, and the other two arrived during the hours of darkness. A rest area had been set up to the rear of the 2nd Battalion administrative area. Here hot chow and a respite from the full day of combat awaited the riflemen of the 1st Battalion, 15th Infantry Regiment. Later, about 2200 hours, the 1st Battalion would move forward and occupy the MLR positions vacated by the 3rd Battalion, which had moved into regimental reserve.

The disposition of the troops on Kelly was substantially different as compared to the previous arrangement on 28 July 1952. Prior to the twenty-eighth, the fortification of Kelly was designed to accommodate a platoon. Now an entire company of infantry had been on the hill since 0815 hours, and the defenses were adjusted to meet the added strength. Captain Neilson placed his 3rd Platoon in the original entrenchment, and the remainder of the company was strung out over a line of one hundred yards along the spine of Kelly. The riflemen were in firing pits on both sides of the spine on the military crest. Newly strung barbwire, placed earlier in the day, formed a protective barrier. Sergeant First Class Henry H. Burke, 3rd Platoon, later said that from a bird's-eye view, the entrenchment resembled a dog collar with an extended leash trailing to the rear.[15]

Outpost Kelly was retaken and in the hands of the U.S. Army. The price had been high, however. Entries on the morning report of 4 August 1952 for the three line companies of the 1st Battalion reported the phrase "heavy enemy contact" and listed the casualties incurred on 31 July 1952. In summary the lists showed the following:

Casualties—31 July 1952

Company	Killed in Action	Severely Wounded	Lightly Wounded	Lightly Injured	Total
A	3	6	14	2	25
B	2	2	12	—	16
C	4	1	21	2	28
Total	9	9	47	4	69

EIGHTEENTH DAY, 2000 HOURS

When the telephone conference call net shut down at 1800 hours, I knew I had an administrative task before me. The S-3, 2nd Battalion, needed my input for the after-action report he must prepare. I collected my thoughts on the happenings of the day and made a mental note of the ones I knew he would need for his report. My contribution could be phoned in, but I wanted to touch base with Holt before the day ended, so I decided to satisfy each requirement with a walk down the hill. I told Gardner where I could be found and took off in the mud. It did not seem to be quite as sticky and clinging as it was at 0430 hours. Or was I imagining the changed condition? I made my way to the S-3 bunker through a lot of troops who were both coming and going. Truck traffic during the day had created some large and deep mud puddles. Casualties were still coming in to the medical aid station. One small bit of relief was the absence of rain; we had been rain free for ten hours. I made my way into the Operations bunker and found myself third in line to see Major Alphson. The line moved quickly, and I soon reported, "Sir, I'm here with my after-action data."

"Siewert, I'm glad to see you!" He looked tired, but he was smiling. "What have you got for me?" The report he was preparing would be consolidated at 15th Regiment with the reports of the other battalions. This information, in turn, would be condensed and integrated and form the basis for the monthly command report. The command report was a strenuously abbreviated narrative, in terse military prose, of significant events that had occurred during the reporting period. I could visualize my platoon data being swallowed and ground up in the integration process.

"The platoon fired 109 rounds. Fifteen were WP on Hill 317, and the remainder was HE plus one more WP on Kelly. My Two-Two tank was disabled before the fight started, so all those rounds went through the Two-One tank gun tube. We commenced firing at 0730 and completed at 0810 hours." I paused while he made note of my comment.

"Wait a minute," he said. "One hundred and nine rounds fired by one tank? How long did you say, forty minutes? A tank doesn't have that many rounds. How did you do that? I'm no tanker, but I know that the ammo is under the floor of the turret. Bob Fowler [Captain Robert E. Fowler, CO, B Company] was on the phone a little while ago about the relief of Kelly tonight. In passing he said the tank HE was hitting Kelly at a hell of a rate. How did you get the rounds out of the floor that fast?"

"I don't know if I should tell you how it was done. There is no doctrine that I know of that prescribes what I did. I could be getting myself in hot water."

"Come on, let me have it," he said. "You're sure as hell not going to get in trouble for what you did today. Bob Fowler swears by your tanks."

"Well, my tank had one hundred rounds stacked like cordwood on the back deck," I said. I then explained the "bucket brigade" process and steam off the barrel. I finished by saying, "We got lucky when the rain stopped because it gave my gunner a clear look at Kelly through the telescope. We were putting out rounds at six to eight per minute for a short while. There was a risk with the rounds stacked out in the open, but I wasn't going to repeat the situation I had when supporting the platoon from Fox Company on the twenty-ninth."

"Siewert, that is one hell of a story. It'll go in my report to Regiment." He was grinning at the thought. "What else have you got?"

"Just some statistics. You know about the disabled tank and the rain. Well, the Two-One tank bunker collapsed from all the rain. We've had mortars coming at us for two weeks—what the Chinese couldn't accomplish, the rain demolished."

"Yeah," he replied, "I've already got reports of over thirty collapsed bunkers in the 2nd Battalion sector. I'll bet Regiment will tally over a hundred by the time the command report is finalized."[16]

"That's about all I have." I saluted and started to turn to leave.

"Take care of yourself—you look played out," he said with an emphatic nod of his head. "Your tank fire had a big part in getting Kelly back—good work!"

Played out or not, I had a good feeling as I left the bunker. It was the kind you get when you know that your presence at an event made a real difference. That kind of feeling does not happen too often in your life.

At the tank perimeter I brought Holt up to date. There was not much he did not already know. I had purposely left my intercom hand mike switch on open all day; this put him in on everything said in the turret via the SCR-508 radio net. Then it was his turn to bring me up to date—with an unexpected surprise.

"Around noontime I released two men from each crew to assist in bringing in the casualties." He paused, trying to gauge my reaction, and then continued, "Hell. We've been sitting here for three weeks, pretty much doing nothing. The men wanted to be part of the attack in some way. This was our contribution," he ended, almost defiantly.

"Where?" I asked, holding my breath. My first thought was what would happen if a crewman was injured—would it be in the line of duty?

"Oh. They went just forward of the MLR, where the KSCs bring the wounded from Kelly and 164. It's like a relay station. I waited until there wasn't much likelihood of getting caught in a firefight or a mortar concentration. I put Sergeant Andy Verducci in charge. All of them are back already—they're exhausted. Climbing up and down ridges, holding the corner of a litter, is tough duty." He finished and waited.

By this time I had sorted out my response. As Holt had been speaking I had gone through an emotional tug-of-war. Part of me wanted to applaud, and the other wanted to raise the roof. I decided to applaud. The crewmen had shown a very desirable quality—high morale and spirit. They did not want to sit on the sidelines; they wanted to be part of the action. They had sought and found an avenue to make a contribution, and for this they deserved commendation, not criticism.

"Sergeant, you made a good decision," I said with a smile. "An aggressive attitude should be encouraged, and you did that by sending those men forward. But no more trips beyond the MLR. I don't want to have to report an injured crewman to Captain Barrett."

Before the day was out, I had spoken to each crew. I addressed Holt's group first and then the two crews on the hill. The main point I stressed was the pride I took in their team performance from the day we arrived to today's successful assault on Kelly. We, as a platoon had accomplished much. Even sitting in the rain day after day, we had made a contribution because we were there—we were ready to perform our mission. And, finally, once in a great while you get to take part in an action where your performance really does make a difference. We, as a platoon, had done it all—and we could stand tall in that knowledge.

It was getting dark when I had the "21" and "22" crews drape camouflage netting over the tanks. As I watched this activity, I looked out at the familiar outline of Kelly fading in the dusk, and a curious thought struck me. Over the past eighteen days we had taken the enemy under fire many times, and yet not once—not even once—had I actually seen him.

The day was Thursday, 31 July 1952—army payday. It was a payday I would never forget.

7
Return to Home Station

NINETEENTH DAY, 0530 HOURS

Sleeping in the hex tent made for tight quarters, but it was manageable, and after several weeks of bunker living, the light and airy tent was a nice change of pace. Overnight, the Chinese artillery and mortar firing had subsided all along our front. Outpost Kelly experienced no hostile action during the night. The first of August started with broken clouds and became brighter as the day went on.

I elected to keep the tanks under camouflage but decided we needed to put the ammunition stowed outside the tanks back into the ammunition wells in the fighting compartment floors. I had reflected last night on the disabled tank situation we had faced the previous morning. Had I left the tanks in their revetments rather than putting them in defilade to avoid attracting attention, there would not have been a disabled tank problem. I was not about to repeat that scenario. The tanks would remain in their revetments except for routine maintenance. I would live, learn, and move on.

I had received no word on the plan of action for this day. I was sure a plan was in the making, and I figured I would probably hear from 2nd Battalion later in the day. There had been no hostile activity since sundown the previous night. Scanning Hill 164 with my binoculars, I could detect no enemy activity or movement. It was quite different at Outpost Kelly. There was movement on the south slope and activity on the crest.

I could not make out what the activity was, but it had to be related to improving the defenses.

At noon a large party of KSCs came up the hill with supplies. The lead group was carrying five-gallon water cans and C ration cartons. At the tail of the column were about two dozen men carrying 4.2-inch mortar rounds in their protective fiberboard cases, one round per man. The destination of the rounds was the 15th Infantry Regiment Heavy Mortar Company. I felt like a neglected poor relation as I watched the rounds go up the road. The two tanks on the hill were down to about half a basic load, perhaps forty rounds in each tank. On the return trip down the hill, a group of the KSCs stopped at the "21" area to salvage the timbers from our collapsed bunker. They were industrious and made short work of removing the timbers from the sandbags and other debris. I had the impression that this bunker was not to be rebuilt. If it was to be rebuilt, I reasoned, why remove the building materials? The muddy road was improving after a twenty-four-hour dry spell.

Later in the afternoon I received a call from the S-3. He said that the 15th Infantry Regiment was in a defensive posture and would put out reconnaissance patrols after dark. He also noted that the Chinese had been quiet since sundown the previous day and that their intentions were unknown. He added that Outpost Kelly was secured and defended by G Company. The 1st Battalion had completed its mission and had been relieved when the responsibility for Outpost Kelly was transferred from B Company to G Company. The relief had taken place at 2000 hours on 31 July. The 1st Battalion was now on the MLR, having replaced the 3rd Battalion during the night. My mission to provide direct-fire support for infantry ground combat had not changed. Major Alphson then asked whether I had any questions. I expressed my concern about the short supply of tank ammunition on hand. He stated he would look into it, and that closed our conversation.

I called Holt on the phone and filled him in on my conversation with the S-3. It turned out that Holt already knew the details, plus he had some information for me. "There was a lot of marching and counter-marching down here yesterday," he said. "First Able Company came through during the day, around noon, marching to a rest area near the ammunition dump. Then, a little after 2000 hours, both Baker and

Charlie companies came marching through to the rest area. Then the 3rd Battalion came off the MLR heading to the rear. That was about 2200 hours. No sooner had they passed when the 1st Battalion came back again to take over the MLR vacated by the 3rd Battalion. Talk about it being busy!"

Sitting up on Hill 199 I had been unaware of all the maneuvering. "The way you describe it, Baker Company must be just below our tank guns. Thanks for the information," I said, as we closed our conversation.[1]

The contrast of this quiet day with the busy, heated activities of the previous day was striking. My day closed with the ever-present question: When do we get off this hill?

TWENTIETH DAY, 0600 HOURS

The sound of construction activity down the road brought a stir to the "21" crew. It was early morning, but something was afoot about a third of the way down the hill. A road gang was in the process of putting our broken road back in order. After breakfast I walked down to the construction site; the workers had set up where the cascading water from the monsoon rains had eroded the surface and washed away a large segment of the road. When I got there they were building a retaining wall on the downslope side of the road. At a glance I figured out where our salvaged bunker timbers went yesterday. A Corps of Engineers sergeant was in charge. His directions to the road gang were relayed through a Korean interpreter. After a short while of observing the work, I concluded that this work gang had done this type of construction before. At the rate the wall was going up, the eroded section would be ready by noontime for the base of riprap to fill the soft bottom; then would come the large aggregate stone, to be finished with fine aggregate. This was a smooth operation. The road repair would be complete before supper if the lower part of the road could handle the truckloads of fill to be brought in. More power to them, I thought, as I returned to the "21" area.

The relief of the 2nd Platoon was dependent on the condition of the roads in the I Corps area. Track-laying vehicles would not move until I

Corps lifted the restrictions that it had instituted a week ago. Road repair here and everywhere in the I Corps area was a part of the equation.

Late in the morning of 2 August 1952, the executive officer, Major Morrison, called and stated that the battalion commander wished to see me at 1130 hours. At the CP bunker I was met by Major Morrison, who said that the CO would see me in a few minutes. A quick look around the bunker showed every indication that the 2nd Battalion was back to a relatively routine operating mode. The dynamics of a frontline infantry battalion, in contact with the enemy, was very evident. Right now this battalion was in a routine defensive posture, and its activities took on a routine, administrative, orderly character. Two days ago "routine" and "orderly" would have been the last descriptive words used to characterize the activities of the battalion. It was not that drive and will and direction were not present in the retaking of Kelly, but the pace of events tumbling one on the other created a very chaotic environment. Urgency and rapid response to cascading events that carried a strong overtone of life and death led to decisions made under great stress. The rules of cause and effect governed the combat, with events often beyond the control of the leaders shaping the final result. And the combat dynamic has no shade of gray—it is either black or white. At this moment in the CP bunker the shade was routine—white.

I addressed the CO. "Colonel, Lieutenant Siewert reporting as directed."

"I'm pleased to see you again, Siewert. Jack, isn't it?" Lieutenant Colonel Roye had the manner of someone with good news to spread around. "Stand at ease. I want to personally commend you and your tanks for the fine performance that you gave in the retaking of Kelly. You know, you are under my operational control, but it was the 1st Battalion that had the benefit of your skills. Colonel Mills Hatfield appreciates the contribution of your platoon—I spoke with him this morning. How are you doing up on the hill? I'm sorry I haven't got up there yet to inspect your fields of fire."

"Sir, we're doing fine."

"I have some news for you—you're to be relieved tomorrow and return to your home station. What do you think of that?" He smiled and sat back, waiting for my reply.

"The 2nd Platoon is ready, sir," I said with a wide grin.

"You'll have to get the details from Major Alphson. I'm sending a report of your part of the action on getting Kelly back, through channels, to your battalion commander." He stood up, extended his hand to shake mine, and said, "Good luck to you, Jack. I'm very glad to have had you with us!"

We shook hands. I stepped back, saluted, and said, "The 2nd Platoon and I thank you, sir! And good-bye."

At the Operations bunker Major Alphson outlined the coming relief. Tanks from the 15th Infantry Regiment Tank Company were expected to arrive in the 2nd Battalion area at 0700 on 3 August. When they were on hand, my two tanks on Hill 199 were to retire from the top of the hill and join my other three tanks; the transfer of responsibility would then be completed. He said he had been told that the road on Hill 199 would be ready for traffic before dark. The motor march of the 2nd Platoon to our home station would be at my discretion. The 64th Tank Battalion had been advised of the relief and return of the 2nd Platoon. Special road clearance and convoy escort would not be required.

We chatted a bit about the fight for Kelly, and then the S-3 said, "Siewert, it's chow time. Why don't we go over to the mess tent and see what they have for lunch?"

"Sounds good to me," I said. "I've been on C rations for a week!"

After lunch I got together with Sergeant First Class Holt, and we developed our plan for the next day's move. His responsibility would center on preparing the three tanks for the move. He assured me the tanks were topped off with fuel and were ready to go. I emphasized that I wanted a well-policed area left behind, with all foxholes, sanitary fills, and latrines filled in and marked. He indicated that his section of tanks would be ready for inspection when I came off the hill tomorrow. I said that the platoon would move out for Charlie Company as soon as the "21" and "22" tanks had been topped off with fuel.

On my way back up the hill, I noted two 6 × 6 trucks filled with aggregate destined for the road repair. The dump trucks, I thought, must be in use elsewhere in the I Corps area. I was surprised, on my way up the hill, to note that the road surface had become quite firm.

The crews at the top of the hill were primed and ready to go and had been for days. I told the drivers of both tanks to plan the exit of their tanks from the revetment to the road carefully. I wanted no disabled tank to interfere with the move the next day. They were to inspect the road repair later in the day to be sure that it would support the tank traffic.

Outpost Kelly had been quiet for two days. As I turned in for the night, I hoped it would stay quiet. I especially wished for no Chinese mortars on Hill 199.

TWENTY-FIRST DAY, 0530 HOURS

The third of August seemed as if it was going to be hot. At 0530 hours the cool dawn had already been burned away. We will be motoring in the dust in another two days, I thought. Korea was a land of contrasts.

The crews busied themselves with striking camp. There really was not much to be done. The men needed to load the gear on the tanks; fill in the foxholes, sanitary fills, and latrines; wash and shave; eat breakfast; and police up the area. And then we waited for the 15th Tank Company tanks to arrive. By looking south at the camouflaged road, we would see the tanks long before they got to the 2nd Battalion area. The plan was to maneuver the "21" and "22" tanks onto the road as soon as we saw the tanks in the distance.

Around 0645 hours the first of two tanks emerged from the camouflage netting. Right on time, I thought. I used the direct telephone line to call Holt and tell him the relief tanks were on their way in. The crews of the "21" and "22" tanks backed the vehicles out of their revetments and parked them in the road. It was a little after 0700 hours when Holt called and said the two tanks of the 15th Tank Company were at the foot of the hill. The transfer was complete. The next step was to return to our home station.

The men of the 2nd Platoon had earned their pay for the month of July. We had been up front, on the line, for twenty-one days. It was certainly a lot longer than we had planned. And now we were coming off Hill 199 to return to Charlie Company—a short one-hour motor march away. It seemed as though we had been in another world for three weeks. I guess, in a sense, we had. And in that time we, the members of the platoon, had become different persons. At least I had. I had come up the hill with a combative, arrogant attitude—"Die Bastards, Die . . . " But that was a long time ago, and I was much older now and somehow changed. My perspective had shifted. Living, and enduring, as an infantryman for three weeks had shown me another side of combat. My plans and expectations had gone through a series of diminishing returns from the initial reconnaissance to the retaking of Outpost Kelly. I was humbled by the experience of initially expecting to put five tanks on the line and ending up with only one tank capable of bringing its gun to bear on the enemy during the final assault on Kelly. My will and desire and determination had been frustrated and reduced, step by step, by circumstance—events I could not control. It had been a sobering learning experience. The platoon mission of "a few days" had stretched to three weeks. We had come full circle and were now returning to our home station.

The "22" tank was first in line, and I watched it make its way slowly down the hill. As a parting gesture, I intended to be the last tank off Hill 199. I had led the platoon up—I would be the last down. Standing in the turret I looked about me. There was the ruined bunker and the Chinese mortar craters downslope, still half-filled with water. And sixteen hundred yards from the crest of Hill 199 was Outpost Kelly, a small feature on the terrain, representing a value in human cost beyond calculation.

Over the intercom I said to Davis, "O.K. Let's take Two-One down." As the tank slowly maneuvered down the road, I glanced about me once again and thought of the deadly toll that Outpost Kelly had exacted. Who was to say it had been worth the cost? Who was to say it had not been worth the cost? I had posed an open question that I would wrestle with for the rest of my life.

Epilogue

The events of those three weeks in July 1952 occurred more than fifty-four years ago. I have forgotten many of the details, yet I was surprised at how much remained to be brought back to the surface of my memory. Although the memories remained dormant for many years, the stimulus of concentration on the chronology brought back events and even fragments of conversations. With the long view of time for my perspective, I believe my understanding of those events is clearer and more intense now than it was fifty-four years ago.

In December 1952 the 3rd Infantry Division awarded me a combat decoration, the Bronze Star Medal (Meritorious). The citation that accompanied the medal summed up, in a brief paragraph, what has taken me many pages to depict in this story. In six sentences the U.S. Army captured the entire thrust of Outpost Kelly. The operative phrase of the citation is "so that he might be with his platoon to direct supporting fire for the infantry as they assaulted an enemy position referred to as 'OP Kelly.'" The phrase inferred a military victory, the retaking of a hill held by the Chinese. In July 1952, a victory at Outpost Kelly was a rational conclusion. Years later, I have acquired a more comprehensive understanding of the Korean War, and today I ask: How meaningful was the victory on Kelly that day? An enemy position was assaulted and secured, but to what end? Outpost Kelly had been lost on 28 July 1952 and retaken on 31 July 1952. We got the hill back—temporarily. On 18 September 1952, the 65th Infantry Regiment lost control of the hill, which is yet another story. Outpost Kelly was never retaken. The hill had been contested three times in the first nine months of 1952. Time and again I have reflected on this give-and-take, and, in my view, Walter G. Hermes has summarized it best: "Unlike all the previous wars waged by the United States, the conflict in Korea brought no military victory; in fact during the last two years of the struggle neither side sought to settle the issue decisively on the battlefield. In this respect the Korean War had no modern American counterpart."[1]

Today, more than half a century later, we still have forty thousand troops manning the front line of the demilitarized zone separating North and South Korea. Who won? Who lost? What are we to conclude? Was Outpost Kelly some sort of political football? Was Kelly a pawn in an international game that is still being played by politicians and statesmen? I did not know then, and I still do not. Outpost Kelly is a minor footnote to the military history of the U.S. armed forces in Korea. We were there for three years, 1950 to 1953, in a conflict that was termed a "police action" to preserve the sovereignty of the Republic of Korea. More than thirty-three thousand U.S. personnel died. More than 103,000 suffered wounds. More than five thousand are still missing. In this perspective Outpost Kelly fades to relative insignificance—or does it?

What are we to make of it? My dilemma is that, on a personal level, I cannot turn my back on Outpost Kelly and just walk away from it. That hill is not insignificant to me. The events that took place on that forlorn hill are seared into my memory. There was a lot of blood and death and agony at the outpost. For a brief moment in time, the "21" tank created a living hell on that hilltop. Now, fifty-four years later, hardly anyone ever heard of the place. The Korean War is a vague historical event that occurred a long time ago in a place far away.

Intuitively, I know that Outpost Kelly should have a meaning, and I am still trying to sort it out. I know that my life has been deeply touched. What occurred on Hill 199 and Outpost Kelly has been a steering force in the direction my life has taken. I am at a loss, however, to explain precisely how my life has been influenced. Regardless, I am aware of how this influence has manifested itself. In a unique way every battlefield is now my battlefield. When I am a visitor standing on the site of a historic battlefield, the significance of the conflict that transpired there brings tears to my eyes. Old memories flood to the surface of my consciousness. I recall the events that occurred at Outpost Kelly. I know what happened at the outpost. All the primal emotions of mankind—fear and anger and hope—were there. It was the same at the "Angle" at Gettysburg and Redoubt Number 10 at Yorktown: conflict; a mutual experience; a common ground. It is my battlefield. This kinship approaches a religious connotation; I feel a reverence, certainly, for hallowed ground bought at the highest price in human values.

The who, what, why, when, and where have faded on these fields, but a salient element stands out—duty. Great deeds, tragic loss of life and suffering, and the ebb and flow of success and failure are products of the attribute of duty. And the binding agent is a band of brothers caught up in the maelstrom of conflict. Why do men advance in the face of fire when they are scared to death, or hold ground against insurmountable odds? When you analyze it and wring it all out, the bottom line is always the brotherhood of a shared experience, an allegiance to the buddy on your right and left—and a sense of duty.

My reaction to battlefields is a sign that tells me that Outpost Kelly was a defining moment in my life. When I came off Hill 199, I knew my life had been altered. I was a different person. The links between life, death, and duty were forged in that long-forgotten fight. Duty, and my understanding of it, is the common ground I share with all battlefields. Some of us live on, and others perish in the fight, but either way duty is the attribute that defines us.

I have one tangible connection to Outpost Kelly—my combat decoration and the citation that goes with it. To be recognized for directing supporting fire for the infantry as they assaulted an enemy position is a great source of pride. It places me in the company of men I greatly admire.

My intangible connection to Outpost Kelly is the knowledge that my being there, in that fight, made a difference. Duty placed the 2nd Platoon, Charlie Company, on that battlefield. As a team, we did our level best to support the infantry carrying the brunt of the assault. The hill was retaken, and our tank fire contributed to the conquest. That, in summary, is probably all I will ever be able to make out of the meaning of Outpost Kelly.

Notes

PREFACE

1. Walter G. Hermes, *Truce Tent and Fighting Front* (Washington, D.C.: U.S. Army, Office of the Chief of Military History, 1966), 507.
2. Ibid., 176.
3. Ibid., 75.

CHAPTER 2

1. Hermes, *Truce Tent and Fighting Front*, 303.
2. Max Hastings, *The Korean War* (New York: Simon and Schuster, 1987), 274.
3. Robert W. Black, *Rangers in Korea* (New York: Ivy Books, 1989), 79.

CHAPTER 3

1. Hastings, *Korean War*, 281.
2. Ibid., 232–33.
3. Hermes, *Truce Tent and Fighting Front*, 181.
4. Ibid., 350.
5. Army Historical Foundation, *The Army* (Westport, Conn.: Hugh Lauter Levin Associates, 2001), 255.
6. "Headquarters, 15th Infantry Regiment, Command Report No. 22, July 1952," part 2(a), National Archives and Records Administration, College Park, Md., 2.

CHAPTER 4

1. "Headquarters, 15th Infantry Regiment, Command Report No. 22," 2.
2. John T. Burke, conversation with author, 19 March 2004.

3. "Headquarters, 15th Infantry Regiment, Command Report No. 22," part 2(b), 8.

4. Ibid.

5. "Morning Report," Headquarters and Headquarters Company, 1st Battalion, 15th Infantry Regiment, National Personnel Records Center, St. Louis, Mo., 3 August 1952.

6. "Headquarters, 15th Infantry Regiment, Command Report no. 22," part 2(b), 8.

CHAPTER 5

1. Sherwin Arculis, letter to author, 31 March 2004.

2. "Headquarters, 15th Infantry Regiment, Journal, Entry Serial No. 166, 1630 hours, 29 July 1952," National Archives and Records Administration.

3. Burke, conversation with author, 24 January 2005.

4. "Headquarters, 15th Infantry Regiment, Journal, Entry Serial No. 166, 1630 hours, 29 July 1952."

5. Ibid.

6. Burke, conversation with author, 19 March 2004.

7. "Headquarters, 15th Infantry Regiment, Command Report No. 22," part 2(a), 3.

8. Ibid.

9. Ibid.

CHAPTER 6

1. "Headquarters, 15th Infantry Regiment, Journal, Entry Serial No. 168, 1640 hours, 29 July 1952."

2. "Headquarters, 15th Infantry Regiment, Journal, Entry Serial No. 160, 1430 hours, 29 July 1952."

3. "Headquarters, 15th Infantry Regiment, Journal, Entry Serial No. 168, 1640 hours, 29 July 1952."

4. "Headquarters, 15th Infantry Regiment, Command Report No. 22," part 2(a), 2.

5. Ibid.

6. "Morning Report," A Company, 15th Infantry Regiment, 3 August 1952.

7. "Headquarters, 15th Infantry Regiment, Command Report No. 22," part 2(a), 4.

8. Ibid.

9. Theodore A. Cook, conversation with author, 22 March 2004.

10. Ibid., 24 January 2005.

11. "Headquarters, 15th Infantry Regiment, Command Report No. 22," part 2(a), 4.

12. Ibid.

13. "Morning Report," Company C, 1st Battalion, 15th Infantry Regiment, 29 July 1952.

14. "Headquarters, 15th Infantry Regiment, Command Report No. 22," part 2(a), 4.

15. Henry H. Burke, conversation with author, 25 March 2004. Burke had made a sketch of the hilltop defense.

16. Rain caused 127 bunkers to collapse. See "Headquarters, 15th Infantry Regiment, Command Report No. 22," part 2(b), 8.

CHAPTER 7

1. "Morning Report," A, B, and C Companies, 15th Infantry Regiment, Record of Events Section, 4 August 1952.

EPILOGUE

1. Hermes, *Truce Tent and Fighting Front*, ix.

Glossary of Terms and Acronyms

CO	Commanding officer.
CP	Command post.
C rations	Combat rations—prepackaged meals of canned goods.
Defilade	Fortification, or natural cover, to provide protection from frontal or enfilading fire. With a hull defilade, the hull of the tank is below ground level, and only the turret is exposed.
EE-8 telephone	A portable telephone developed by the Signal Corps and operated by flashlight-sized batteries. This rugged instrument was designed for use in field conditions. The telephone was used in all theaters of war during World War II and Korea.
FO	Forward observer—an artillery officer assigned to a combat unit to direct artillery fire.
Fuse settings	Term used to refer to the two adjustments for tank high-explosive fuses; the two kinds are "super-quick" and "fuse delay."
Gunners quadrant	An instrument used for indirect-fire adjustment of a cannon.

H&I	Harassing and interdiction fire—usually from artillery and mortar fire. The purpose is to create uncertainty and confusion.
HE	High explosive—a shell that detonates with great explosive force.
Hex tent	A hexagonal-shaped waterproof tent designed to provide temporary shelter for five men.
Hill 199 (and Hill 317 and so on)	A terrain feature, hill, or mountain 199 meters above sea level (other features, hills, and mountains given similar designations).
IP	Initial point—a geographic location, such as a crossroad or row of trees bordering a field, that provides a place or line of departure.
KSC	Korean Service Corps—a South Korean labor force created to support United Nations military units.
Lightly injured in action	An injury other than a wound caused by an enemy weapon.
Lightly wounded in action	An injury that may not require hospitalization; wound is caused by enemy weapon.
LP	Listening post—a small group of men set up to provide early warning of an approaching force. They will often engage the approaching force with small-arms fire to halt or stall an advance.
M-46	Main battle tank of the U.S. Army in Korea. Known as the "Patton," this forty-eight ton, track-laying vehicle was powered by a Continental V-12, 810-horsepower engine and was protected by four inches of frontal armor. The main gun was a 90m/m cannon. The tank had a radius of action of seventy miles. A five-man crew operated the tank.
Mil	Artillery term used to express an angular mea-

surement. There are 6,400 mils in a circle. At one thousand yards the chord of the arc of one mil will subtend a distance of one yard. At two thousand yards the distance would be two yards, and so on.

MLR — Main line of resistance—a concentration of the main force of a military unit, usually fortified.

Motor stables — Routine maintenance performed to ensure the mechanical soundness of the tanks.

MSR — Main supply route.

NCO — Noncommissioned officer.

Net — Network.

OP — Outpost—a military detachment thrown out by a halted command to protect against enemy enterprises.

OPLR — Outpost line of resistance.

Police up — To make clean and put in order. Term describes the activity or action to restore an unacceptable condition or appearance to one that meets the correct standard (e.g., police up the trash on the parade ground).

PRC-10 — Portable field radio used by the infantry.

Quarter-ton truck — A small four-wheel drive truck with a quarter-ton carrying capacity. Also called a "jeep."

R&R — Rest and recuperation.

S-1 — The personnel unit at battalion and regimental levels; also used to refer to the personnel officer.

S-2 — The intelligence unit at battalion and regimental levels; also used to refer to the intelligence officer.

S-3 — The operations unit at battalion and regimental levels; also used to refer to the operations officer.

S-4	The logistics unit at battalion and regimental levels; also used to refer to the logistics officer.
SCR-300	Radio used for communication with units other than tanks (e.g., infantry).
SCR-508	A vehicle-mounted radio for communication between tanks.
Severely wounded in action	An injury that requires hospitalization; wound is caused by enemy weapon.
6 × 6 truck	A six-wheel drive truck with a two-and-one-half-ton carrying capacity; also called a "deuce-and-a-half."
TOT	Time on target—a timed firing in which the shell trajectory from each artillery piece, far or near to the target, is calculated so that the explosive shells arrive at the target simultaneously.
WP	White phosphorus—a shell with white phosphorus used for marking a target or temporarily obscuring a target.

Bibliography

Although much of this volume was written from personal recollection of events that took place in Korea from 1951 to 1952, other sources have also made a valuable contribution to the story.

PRIMARY SOURCES

The National Archives and Records Administration, College Park, Maryland, provided the document "Headquarters, 15th Infantry Regiment, Command Report Number 22, July 1952." This document was most useful in establishing the time, date, place, and unit involved in the combat action. The National Archives also provided several pages of entries made on 29 July 1952 of the "15th Infantry Regiment Journal." This document recorded daily events on a sequential minute-by-minute basis. Entries included incidents, messages, orders, and so on.

The National Personnel Records Center, St. Louis, Missouri, provided "Morning Reports" for companies of the 7th Infantry Regiment, 15th Infantry Regiment, and the 64th Tank Battalion. These reports reflected the personnel activities of the unit, including daily company unit strength, casualties, record of events, location, and unit troop movement.

Personal conversations with soldiers who were present on the battlefield during the period 28–31 July 1952 provided individual accounts and anecdotes of their combat experience.

Letters to my wife, Loel J. Siewert, covering the period October 1951 to September 1952, were carefully preserved as a family heritage. The contents of these seventy-five letters provided a chronology of my service experience and included details of persons, places, and events relevant to the story of Outpost Kelly.

SECONDARY SOURCES

The following books made a substantial contribution to the story by providing a literary reference to events that took place in Korea from 1951 to 1952.

Army Historical Foundation. *The Army*. Westport, Conn.: Hugh Lauter Levin Associates, 2001.

Black, Robert W. *Rangers in Korea*. New York: Ivy Books, 1989.

Dolcater, Max W., ed. *Third Infantry Division in Korea*. Tokyo: Toppan Printing, 1953.

Hastings, Max. *The Korean War*. New York: Simon and Schuster, 1987.

Hermes, Walter G. *Truce Tent and Fighting Front*. Washington, D.C.: U.S. Army, Office of the Chief of Military History, 1966.